ARE YOU THE LEADER YOU WANT TO BE?

MANBIR KAUR
with KATHY MITCHELL

Happy Reading!

Manlui

First Edition: January 2018
Printed in India

ISBN: 978-93-87269-37-8
Cover Design: Team StoryMirror

STORYMIRROЯ
Stories that reflect you

Publisher: StoryMirror Infotech Pvt. Ltd.
                  1108, 11th Floor, Pragati Tower,
                  Rajendra Place, New Delhi - 110008
                  145, First Floor, Powai Plaza,
                  Hiranandani Gardens, Powai - 400076,
                  Mumbai , India

Web: www.storymirror.com
Facebook: www.facebook.com/storymirror
Twitter: https://twitter.com/story_mirror
Instagram: https://instagram.com/storymirror

What Leaders and Experts are saying about
"Are You the Leader You Want to Be ?"

ARE YOU THE LEADER YOU WANT TO BE? is an excellent and insightful read by Kathy and Manbir. The HUMAN model addresses the complex challenges faced by most growing technology firms in a unique and simple manner. The narrative methodology provides us with a step by step way to engage and lead our teams in the most productive and effective way. I would strongly recommend this book to current and potential leaders in technology organisations- both startups and multinationals.

Ankit Agarwal
Director , Sterlite Technologies Ltd.

A vast majority of businesses as per various studies continue to fall short on 'Leadership and Employee engagement' either due to a lack of correct understanding or right execution. I am happy to refer this experiential and handy book authored by an interesting duo, Manbir and Kathy who 'have been there and done that' in business world . Manbir has been an outstanding business leader while kathy is a 'people champion' who helps enable businesses to succeed by providing the vital link of aligning and engaging people to accomplish productivity and business goals.

Engagement is a two way collaborative process. The authors in this refreshingly simple book filled with live examples offer a very realistic and easy to apply "HUMAN" framework in a conversational story format. As a technology business leader, this engaging book is very practical & serves like a ready reckoner to me. I would very positively recommend the same to all Business/ HR leaders of Tech organisations, who aim to winningly align their strategic aims with people development and engagement.

Vijay Rai
Managing Director-Enterprise Business Asia Pacific &
EMEA Markets, Saviour US INC. &
President - NHRDN Delhi & NCR Chapter

Organisational landscapes today are littered with case studies of corporate leaders failing to engage and motivate their workforce. The tech sector is particularly in focus, going through a public and difficult "growing-up" and what worked in the last two decades is being rapidly replaced with newer practices, models and approaches, especially when it comes to the discipline of employee engagement.

In this context, "Are You The Leader You Want To Be" by Manbir Kaur & Kathy Mitchell is a timely intervention, providing a fresh perspective and simple, yet penetrating insights on this critical topic. Set-out in classical case-study format, the book provides an instantly usable framework, enabling the reader to create in a practical way a roadmap of interventions and initiatives and the 'how-to' guide to implement them.

With their own years of experience at the coal face of tech and HR, the authors have given an invaluable tool in every new leader's toolkit.

Amit Dhawan
Investor & Entrepreneur

In certain circles within technology, people argue that leadership skills impact every part of a company's eco-system. Some argue that a frightening majority of management leadership are not engaged. This is a book that will present the data and present key factors of a leadership framework in a step by step, digestible manner. Business success in this age is based upon books that present clear, data driven frameworks, tips and things to avoid. Here is a wonderful guide to gaining that competitive edge.

Michael Rawlins,
User Experience Strategist,
ESPN/ Walt Disney Company

An interesting take at inspirational leadership – and a guide to find your inspiration style – especially if leadership models sound like gobbledegook to the 'techie' you. The authors present a simple model and elucidate the same using tales from a mythical tech firm. One can't but reflect, how many Arun's fumble through the corporate maze – struggling to tap into their purpose, struggling to inspire teams and looking for a magical wand that will unleash the true potential of the business and their teams! 'HUMAN' is just that - a "no fluff" wand for all Arun's in and around us!

Mahalakshmi R.
Senior HR Leader

In my long career in the technology sector I have seen many highly successful individual contributors struggle to deliver when promoted to managerial roles.

The reason for this is not difficult to understand. In technical roles, they had worked on well-defined problems, in a structured environment with plenty of inputs available on how to deliver on the tasks assigned to them. But when they became team leaders, they were thrown out of this comfort zone and had to cope with the complexities of team dynamics as well as uncertainties of business – two challenges that they were never trained for.

This book promises to boost the career of professionals with a technology background by giving them a simple HUMAN framework for effective leadership of teams that consistently delivers results in an ever-changing business environment.

Ravi Chauhan
Founder - The Leadership Consulting

As an experienced leader, responsible for delivering on critical and important objectives, relationships are at the helm of achieving success with grace. People sit at the center of our success and the HUMAN framework will make it easy to ensure valuable engagement and alignment.

Manbir and Kathy have strung "pearls of wisdom" in this book you hold. Buy it and use it. It's worth your while!!

Swati Rangachari
Chief Corporate affairs
Sterlite Technologies Limited.

In the ever-changing technological landscape, coupled with today's businesses operational and transformation challenges, what has worked yesterday may or will not work for today or tomorrow's teams. How does one navigate these challenges and find the right path or spirit to motivate, inspire & drive their teams towards excellence?

This book answers many of these questions faced by many of us today and provides a real step by step approach to solve many of these invisible problems & challenges. Many of us can surely picture ourselves either in the protagonist's shoes or in the mentor's shoes in some of our real-life situations. The powerful HUMAN framework offers principles, studies, and practices to present an innovative step by step structure and approach that strengthens our grasps and deepens our understanding. Story style of presentation of ideas and thoughts eases the complexity of topic and illustrates concepts more visually.

With this book, both Manbir Kaur and Kathy Mitchell have distilled their decades of business leadership experience, human resource leadership experience, many years of executive leadership coaching experiences in large multi-national organisations and offered simple but practical ideas that can work for anyone to be a successful leader in their path.

Nagaraja Upadhya
Telecommunication Executive, USA

Managers of today have a herculean task of not only getting the work completed on time but also keeping the diverse workforce engaged. Gone are the days when the managers could just issue a directive and it was followed in letter and spirit. With the change in the culture and demands coming from millennials and a very diverse workforce, the needs are different today and with different asks, the manager has to have a very different approach for each of them. This book would help them understand the basics and through storytelling and giving live examples which the managers can correlate with from their own lives, both Kathy and Manbir have done an excellent job at making this book practical and very informative and almost like a bible for all managers.

Malvieka Joshi
Senior Director Human Resources
Ciena India Private Ltd, Gurgaon

While moving up the career ladder, technology professionals face a strange situation, where they have to work with multiple teams from diverse functions. Each team look at a project from their own perspective, hence leaders have to answer/convince each team in multiple perspectives, in such situations leaders may lose focus & direction

The concept of HUMAN, will help a technology professional in wading through confusions, uncertainties & paradoxes, who have just entered in to new realm of cross functional, cultural and collaborations.

Fable based framework of HUMAN will help in straddling various facets of a complex problem/situation and aligning, convincing individuals to give their best possible potential to achieve desired results, in the process individuals may attain a better degree of mental, emotional maturity.

Venkat Reddy
Practice Head, Ericsson

For an aspiring leader, this very inviting title of the book leads into a jargon free self- help recipe book on engaged leadership. At the heart of the book is the HUMAN framework so missing in today's bottom line focused and technology led workplace.

The authors encourage the reader to first Heed to their own inner self and then Understand the personalities of the team members. They then encourage us to seamlessly engage the team members through alignment and feedback Messaging with the final goal to Nurture them to be leaders themselves.

Simple conversation style between mentor and protagonist to illustrate the use of HUMAN framework in curated steps makes it handy to internalise the principles and apply. The authors encourage aspiring leaders to get back to basic principles of trust and care on which human civilisation is built and in the process, make the workplace a perfect and happy place for all to contribute and enjoy.

Partha Sarathi
Technical Team Lead, MNC company

In an ever evolving technology sector, product lifecycle has reduced drastically, expectations from executives & leaders are entirely different as compared to a decade back. This book has come at the very right time and it can become an effective tool for executives and leaders to manage high performance team and hence grow in their career ladder. The framework HUMAN conceptualised in this book is really very impressive, simple to understand & adopts practical scenarios in the corporate world of today. This is a must read for leaders and budding leaders in technology organisations.

Chandan Kumar
Director, Marketing and Corporate Affairs , Huawei India

I feel privileged to be asked to write a review on the upcoming book by Kathy and Manbir. They bring their passion, talent and skills as specialists in the technology industry with their background in leadership, consulting and coaching for this book project. The book is a "gem" since it incorporates learning reflections through story telling of real life experiences, a clear framework to adopt and worksheets for practice. What else could you ask for? I congratulate both Kathy and Manbir for making this great contribution to empower leaders in the technology industry through this book. As I went through the contents, I recollect a Gallup study done many years ago that found that at least 70% of the variance in employee engagement scores is driven by who the boss is. This is disconcerting because the same research found that about 70% of people in management roles are not well equipped for the job. This state of affairs is hurting not just employee engagement and quality of life, but also corporate performance. The HUMAN framework introduced in this book will instil the purpose, provide a proven process and provide the opportunity to practice and bring the results that any leader aspires, and thus reducing the gaps in employee engagement and thereby continue to build corporate performance. Enjoy the book and make a difference!

Rajiv Mathews George, PCC
Leadership Coach, Mentor & Supervisor
Harvest Global Resources Sdn.Bhd.

Data has proven that a highly engaged workforce leads to higher customer satisfaction scores, are more likely to refer and build the organisation and are 6% higher in productivity. Employee engagement has always been and continues to be an issue that most organisations in the technology sector have been grappling with. This book provides a practical (HUMAN) approach in addressing this issue and equips managers to move their teams from TGIF syndrome to TGIM! (Thank God It's Monday). Congratulations Manbir and Kathy.

Pallavi Kapoor
Dell , HRBP- India Sales & APJ DCSE

Most leaders are on a journey to improve their impact on their teams. Manbir and Kathy have discovered the threads which improve the effectiveness of leaders, especially in technology organisations. These experienced leaders, developers of leaders, and authors know their own learning and the learning of their team members starts with awareness, builds to understanding, applies approaches to build the leader's own skills, and applies approaches to develop the team members' own skills.

All of this begins with the leader seeing the need to start building the team through relationship and setting direction rather than through just the details of the work itself. People want to work with a clear and noble purpose larger than their own gain. Good leaders use the HUMAN model built by the authors to elevate and motivate. The elevation is team understanding of purpose and goals for the work of the enterprise. The elevation is also the leader's conscious development of both individual and team skills so engagement in this worthwhile work motivates team members and their leaders to consistently put forth discretionary effort previously untapped.

As a leader in a technical organisation, stop to think whether you are focusing on just the job content or inspiring this discretionary effort. Let Manbir and Kathy show you how to read the context of your organisation, express the higher purpose, reveal the engaging elements through effective stories, and celebrate the results of greater engagement and thus discretionary effort.

Their book is a strong reference and guide to my work both as a leader and as a developer of experienced leaders, especially engineers, scientists, and technology professionals. Make their book part of your own development as a leader.

Ken Graham, Ph.D.
Strategy, Leadership, and Change Consultant and
Global Head of Leadership Development (Retired)
Shell Exploration and Production

In my experience in working with current and emerging leaders in organisations across the world, the move from a 'Manager' to a 'Leader' can be complex and difficult. There can be a range of emotions - uncertainty, ambiguity, excitement, pride and of course a strong desire to quickly make an impact. Often though, leaders do not have access to support and advice to help them through this transition. For technology leaders who have been very used to working with information and systems, this transition can be more acute with the need to be visionary, engaging and to inspire and motivate their teams and their organisation.

Manbir and Kathy have created a very workable framework - HUMAN - for technology leaders in this situation. HUMAN is based on in depth research and the experiences that Manbir and Kathy have in working with Leaders experiencing change. I recommend HUMAN as an essential guide for personal development.

Mike Clark
Global Leadership Development specialist
and Executive Coach

In the last couple of decades technologies have significantly evolved at an accelerating pace and together with these changes organisations have mutated from traditional pyramidal structures to smaller but more complex team groups.

New technology and IT business is now almost exclusively project focused, requiring skilled natural leaders to set up and motivate short life teams of individuals often geographically, culturally or technically diverse.

A new generation of managers must learn to bring team members skills and energy together toward a common project/sales goal.

Franck Bertuzzi
APAC SE Director, Ciena

I am happy to read the book by Manbir Kaur and Kathy Mitchell. It is truly introspective as well as forward-thinking.

One of the greatest challenges faced by our world today is that despite all the technology possible, or maybe because of it... despite all the laws and rules set - or maybe because of them... we as humanity are actually losing the HUMAN touch.

In taking forward our corporates and our companies, our NGOs and our Causes, and in fact all our institutions, we forget those who are the most important - our people.

All the very best, Manbir and Kathy, for this wonderful initiative. I hope your book goes to more and more people every day, and awakens many to the evolved thoughts in it. God bless.

Rashmi Anand
Inspirational speaker, Social Worker, Counsellor,
Author of 13 books.

Foreword

We are all confronted with the rapidity of change in just about all aspects of our environment and the challenge of organisations and leadership to deal with these changes effectively. These are empirical facts and don't need much convincing. The authors highlight how the rate of change and its impact on organisations and leadership is particularly acute in technology companies and the additional imperatives this places on Leaders in Technology companies. The importance of motivating Teams to accomplish the goals of the organisation is highlighted. Moving from "Disengaged" to "Engaged Teams", becomes a critical skill for Leaders in Technology companies. Failure to do so has career limiting implications for Leaders and competitive failure for the organisations they lead.

In the book, the authors focus on the critical success factors necessary for Leaders in technology companies to lead successful teams. The acronym used in the book, "HUMAN", encapsulates their articulation of the critical success factors for a Leader.

I found the book an easy read, devoid of the clutter of jargon and bromides. Through a case study approach, using experiential anecdotes, yet conversational, the authors provide both a conceptual and practical approach to development of those leadership traits essential for success in technology companies. The worksheets provided are helpful and provide for focus and articulation of goals to be benchmarked and measured to ensure progress and achievement of goals. I am convinced the book will not only engage the reader but will find the person returning again and again for helpful guidance as they benchmark their way to success! I highly recommend this book to all those aspiring, promising leaders, who take seriously, Marshall Goldsmith's dictum, "What got you here, won't get you there".

Rajan S. Mathews
Director General
COAI (Cellular Operators Association of India)

Acknowledgements

I would like to take this opportunity to thank the universe as well as everybody who touched my life.

This book is a result of more than 20 years of professional experience - learning, practicing, researching and coaching. It has been my good fortune to be professionally associated with leaders from large technology companies. A lot of insights that I present in this book are a result of this association with leaders. I thank you all for the wonderful experiences and the influence you have in my life.

I humbly thank Andrew Neitlich and the Center for Executive Coaching for providing me with great tools and techniques to work with leadership teams and for helping me understand the application of coaching to the business leaders. Thanks Andrew, for also helping me define my own Niche and setting me down the path to develop new models specifically focusing on my clients.

Dear Judith E. Glaser, I am indebted to you and my C-IQ colleagues for their endless support, guidance, and motivation.

I am in gratitude to all my clients for their faith in me. A very humble thanks to the clients who applied the framework in practice. I greatly appreciate your feedback. Your endorsement has been the best reward for all the efforts that I have put in for developing this unique framework.

Dear God, thanks for bringing Kathy Mitchell into my life. Dear Kathy, without your support this book would not have seen the light of the day. Thank you for becoming my alter-ego, a real partner in this whole journey. You brought in a wealth of knowledge and skills that helped shape this book. Your prior experience in HR and leadership development has been invaluable and you have greatly helped in making this book more readable.

I thank all my friends and colleagues who gave me the opportunity to discuss my ideas with them. The debates and discussions helped me sharpen and tune my framework better. These discussions at times have been difficult, and have prompted more study and experimentation. I have personally gone through various stages of development and growth during this journey and these discussions were an essential element.

I also acknowledge my fellow coaches from ICF Delhi NCR Chapter for their support.

Dear Rajan S. Mathews, a very humble thanks to you for an inspiring foreword.

Deep gratitude to Marshall Goldsmith and all the senior industry leaders for reviewing our work and for providing their endorsements for the book. Thanks for your time and kind gesture. For both our readers and ourselves your words are invaluable.

I also thank the team at "Story Mirror", for helping me through this fantastic journey. You made my dream come true by giving life to my Book.

Last but not the least, I thank my husband, Jatinder and son, Ishnoor who stood by me, always supporting and encouraging me. Thanks Jatinder, for burning midnight oil and dedicating many weekends for helping Kathy and me on this project. Without your endless support, I could not have imagined this day.

Manbir Kaur

Acknowledgements

Though the working world is complex, and fast paced, and you wonder if you can ever keep up with the changes, this wonderful environment has thrust Manbir and myself unexpectedly together, two total strangers with a passion for coaching and developing leaders, to produce this book. Manbir is from India and I from Australia and thanks to technology we have forged a lifelong friendship.

I love that I have the opportunity to acknowledge Manbir, the principle author. I want to thank Manbir for choosing me to go on this journey with her, a person never thinking in her wildest dreams she would be involved in writing a book, let alone having a book published. Manbir has had the vision, belief, drive, passion, humbleness, the HUMAN framework and the tenaciousness to keep the book alive and deliver it. Well done dear friend, you did it!

I would like to say a special and big thank you to JP Singh, Manbir's husband. I know that he has been working tirelessly behind the scene supporting us. His wisdom, forethought and experience has been crucial in shaping this book in to what it is today. It will be my honour to meet you and I cannot wait until we meet so that I can thank you in person.

Thank you to Paul Tulip who, in the initial stages of the book, showed interest and kindly took his own personal time to read a few chapters and provide us insightful and helpful feedback. Paul, I wish you even greater success as a leader in technology.

Thank you to our Reviewers for their encouragement and enthusiasm. We are humbled by your willingness to be involved in our book and your review.

I must make specific mention of the amazing Marshall Gold-smith, an inspiring executive coach who wants to make a difference in the world by helping people be a greater version of themselves.   Thank you for helping me too, you have personally touched my life in endorsing our book.

A big thank you to Story Mirror and their team, our Publish-er.   You chose to 'give us a go', two ladies with a dream to help technology leaders be the leader's they want to be. You are making a difference. Thank you.

To my wonderful husband, Keith. Thank you for allowing me to be me and for giving me the space and support to keep exploring. Writing this book has been a journey of exploration, and that what seems impossible is possible. From this experience, I wonder, what next! I am so excited and even more excited because you are with me!

Kathy Mitchell

Preface

Manbir has had the opportunity to be closely associated with the technology sector for many years. This exposure has given her the opportunity to face many of the challenges first hand, and experience the leadership capabilities as well as the limitations of the currently available literature for technology leadership development.

For many years, she was perplexed by the fact that while some of the leaders were really inspiring others were clearly not. She asked herself the question, what made us decide that we love to work for one leader while not for the other? She looked for hints and was intrigued by the fact that the conversations with great leaders were different, they tended to boost you up!

As she started her coaching journey a few years back, she has had the opportunity to work with quite a few organisations and did encounter leaders with varying degrees of success and they all had different styles of leadership. All these encounters kept her wondering about the right combination for a great leader.

In the process of getting further accreditation on coaching, Manbir connected with Andrew Neitlich and his wonderful organisation "Center for Executive Coaching". There she discovered some new concepts that immediately rang a bell with the technologist in her.

She defined her niche under Andrew's guidance. She now has a focussed approach for the technology sector. While working as a coach with technology leaders, she realised that most of them are quite passionate about their work however, when it comes to team engagement, they find it challenging.

Manbir developed the framework "HUMAN", targeted especially at the technology leaders, supporting and helping them to engage and align their teams. She has been able to solidify many of the abstract concepts into simple processes, creating a journey for the technology leader in becoming a great leader.

At the core of her framework is the recognition that technology leaders require a lot more systematic and structured approach. They always want to measure the effectiveness of any course of action, their minds are built to question, they evaluate the efficiency and seek clarity.

Manbir has been practicing this framework over the last few years and has found that it does fit the needs, curiosity and even the exacting standards of clarity that the technology people have.

She had for a long time wanted to share her framework with all technology leaders and started on the idea of this book. At this juncture, Manbir and Kathy met and had a common interest in helping technology leaders. Kathy has first-hand experience of working with technology people as part of HR leadership. She related to the idea easily. Manbir and Kathy started exchanging ideas and continued to evolve and refine the framework. Both were equally passionate about leadership development and acknowledged the lack of specific literature in the technology space.

Kathy Mitchell, with her experience in HR and leadership development, greatly complemented Manbir's experience on the business verticals within technology companies. Together they discussed and developed the concept. Thus, the bones of the book started to take shape. Kathy was the one who was instrumental in helping to decide the current "coaching style" of the book. Together, they have been on this journey for the past three years and the result of their labour is in your hands today.

This book has been written with coaching methodologies in mind. With the help of dialogues between the protagonist and his mentor, they have tried to answer quite a few questions that may come to the mind of a technology leader. This book cannot substitute an actual coach, but presents to you the framework and will definitely help you progress on the path to becoming "The leader you always wanted to be". They hope that the book can help you understand the importance of team engagement as well as alignment, and present to you the tools to achieve it. They hope that the book enhances your own knowledge and hastens your journey to be a great leader. If this book has achieved these two goals, then it has connected with you, the readers!

Contents

Foreword

Acknowledgements

Preface

Introduction

Introduction 31

A Quick Peek 34

Disengagement is the Root Cause 40

Technology Leaders are Conditioned Differently 47

Introduction to HUMAN 52

Story Play 60

Heeding Yourself

H – Heeding Yourself 71

Day 5: The story continues 89

Understanding Your Team

U - Understanding Your Team 109

Know Your Team Members 110

Day 14: The story continues 125

Understand the Role and Create Alignment 131

Day 28: The story continues 136

Messaging

Messages - Using Right Messages and Stories 145

General Messages 148

Day 42: The story continues 155

Feedback 161

Day 56: The story continues 170

Share Stories that Engage and Inspire 176

Day 84: The story continues 181

Acknowledging

Acknowledging 187

Crafting an Acknowledgement Strategy 189

Day 116: The story continues 195

Nurturing

Nurture Team Members 203

Development Planning 206

Day 148: The story continues 218

Conclusion

Conclusion 225

APPENDIX -1

Introduction

"Coming Together is a beginning;
Keeping together is a process;
Working together is success"

-Henry Ford

Introduction

All of us dream, aspire and even chase a perfect workplace. Over the last few decades, our workplaces have undergone huge change. We work in a global setup, and the pace of change is increasing each day. The dynamics of the workplace have become more complex, and it is imperative that decisions are made quickly. The workplace has become VUCA (Volatile, Uncertain, Complex, and Ambiguous) and this is a reality that organisations are working towards accepting and adapting to. Not only are the workplace external drivers different, but also the employees have different behaviours. Employees are looking for that perfect workplace, whereby they have meaning in their work, can see growth opportunities, feel appreciated, and we know they are willing to leave their job in search of this. Under such circumstances, the role of the leaders has become even more important and critical to organisational success.

Diverse teams, which are geographically spread, often work in a complex and fast-paced environment linking employees, organisation and customer issues. All of this results in significant levels of stress and frustration for leaders.

As technologies are evolving faster, the speed of change is even faster for the technology organisations. Technology leaders who lead through change have a very complex responsibility to lead the teams and organisation in the direction it needs to go; to achieve amazing growth and competitive advantage.

When roles expand and technology leaders assume greater

> *In a number of surveys conducted in recent years, it is reported that only 13% to 25% of the workforce feels engaged at work. This shocking result means that the rest of the employees are not engaged.*

accountability and responsibilities, leading bigger teams, more often than not, they feel lost. Technology leaders due to the very special nature of their jobs, develop skills and traits that help them cope better with projects and execution. But quite often than not, they struggle to motivate teams and create synergies and cohesion required to achieve organisational success. They start to understand that they are missing something and feel that there are some invisible problems that exist but are eluding them.

The technology organisations that develop leaders who can lead their people through these constantly changing parameters are likely to be successful and more recognised. These organisations are the ones that will survive.

At the same time, the technology leaders who adapt themselves and are ready and able to navigate the new world order are the ones that organisations will look to lead their businesses and for these technology leaders the career opportunities will be endless.

The need of the hour is to have technology leaders who can work at a higher pace in an agile environment, taking their people along with them.

Where to Find Engaging Leaders?

Leadership is for everyone who is willing to learn, develop and adapt to this new paradigm. Technology leaders must be willing to learn and embrace the principles of engagement. They must develop and lead fully engaged teams that can navigate this new world order. This is a key for leaders in our current workplace.

While there are no silver bullets, there are simple yet powerful leadership practices that are easy to implement, and produce immediate improvements.

Technology leaders can now STOP struggling to engage and motivate their teams and make the teams more aligned and accountable. How? By simply following a step by step, easy and Do It Yourself (DIY) approach.

How Will This Book Help You?

In this book, we have combined various principles, studies, practices to present a path-breaking, no-fluff framework called **HUMAN** which can easily be followed to make *the invisible* visible.

Our framework of engagement leverages the skills and traits that technology people already have. The book provides a step by step approach supported by DIY worksheets and a story that illustrates the framework.

You will discover that real engagement is not rocket science and with focus you can create an engaged, highly performing team and become that leader you always wanted to be. Yes, the one everyone wants to work for!

When teams are engaged, they grow and they become more productive. They deliver in more effective ways and enjoy coming to work. The leader of such a team is recognised and is offered bigger opportunities, more important ones, and hence is able to progress to the next level in his/her career.

In a nutshell, the more you work for your team, develop their skills, and empower them to do the job, the more time and opportunities you will have to work on your own growth and development.

Have you noticed some people taking this route to success? Making you feel that they have an elevator while you are just climbing stairs!

This book shares with you the secrets of such successful people so that you have your own personal elevator to the top floor.

A Quick Peek

Volatility and Technology Organisations

In the new world order, the technology organisations feel the volatility driver on a very high scale as technology changes at a much faster pace. Technologies such as artificial intelligence, machine learning, robotics, autonomous cars, drones etc., which were almost non-existent a few years ago are mainstream technologies today, impacting many a business and jobs.

Even customers of technology organisations change their requirements rapidly, wanting to keep pace with their competitors. Global organisations must keep pace with the changing environment in various geographies, each with different demographics and dynamics of its own. Changes at one location have cascading effects on teams located in other parts of the world.

People in a technology-driven organisation are expected to always develop the best products and services, despite ever-changing technologies with limited scope for failure. They need to keep pace with what is happening outside, in addition to delivering their best. Traits like innovation, problem-solving, decision-making and strategy cannot be the responsibility of just one team but a group of people and teams that need to work collaboratively together. Almost all teams are required to contribute towards achieving the big picture, and simultaneously excelling at their own scope.

In this constantly changing world, great teams continue to

outperform the market. It is the leader's onus to develop and engage teams in such a way that they always come out as winners. However, in our experience, there are many instances, where teams are not able to perform their best; we shall talk about some of these further in the book.

Work Environment in a Technology Organisation

A Few Non-Performing Teams

In our own experience while working with technology companies, we found that quite a few of them struggle to create synergy between people and teams. Also, in most of these organisations, we have found that much of the workforce is not engaged to the fullest potential. Given below are some of the stories we would like to share with you to highlight the scenarios where we found that the teams were disengaged. We are sure that you will relate to at least one of them, if not all.

A. *In one of the cases, when the project team of the company went to implement the project they had just won, they found that some of the customer expectations were unrealistic. They started explaining to the customer why some of the* tasks would take longer and why some were not even necessary to be carried out. The customer was surprised and shared the proposal agreed by their sales team and insisted on this delivery. The project team continued to disown some of the conditions agreed in the contract, and expressed in multiple ways to the customer that their sales team may have made mistakes. Not even one of the team members took ownership of the deliverables. As you can imagine, this whole episode eroded the customer's confidence, and understandably they started to distrust the entire company. It took quite an effort and at times heated discussions within the organisation to return with a plan that aided in meeting the customer needs. These internal discussions were full of mistrust among people. In the end, they overcame all the obstacles. They implemented the project but lost the customer's trust forever. If the company had an environment where teams were fully engaged, the mindset and behaviours seen would have been greatly different. People would have had a proactive approach, demonstrated collective ownership and could have been keen to solve problems from the very start. There would also have been an environment of clear and open communication between the various internal stakeholder teams. Their collaborative behaviour would have helped the company overcome or avoid such issues.

I didn't commit it....

- Unrealistic expectations
- Impossible time targets

- Shared signed agreements
- Purchase Order based on agreements

- Disown deliverables
- Escalates internally and pushes back

- Customer lost confidence
- Heated discussions between stakeholders
- Finally all came together to offer an alternative at additional cost

---

B. *One of the client organisations that we have worked with had a history of delayed deadlines for most of the project milestones from one of their teams. When we discussed the issue, most of the problems were due to team members and sub-teams not communicating effectively with each other. Through further discussion and deeper insights, it appeared that the teams were not engaged enough and also did not understand how their part of the project was instrumental in the overall success of the project.*

> *It was a typical situation of "my work-your work".*
> *"If I have done my job, then I have done my part."*
> *"I am not worried about what other teams do."*

Hence, overall the project was delayed by 50%. Each time they tried to correct the problem, they added one more spreadsheet to a bunch of already existing reporting and measurement effectiveness charts, but nobody fixed the intangible components. The overall situation could have been much better if teams and managers had engaged more openly with each other, sharing what they were doing, and were able to connect their work to the big picture. Unless people own and feel accountable, understand their role and how it supports the success of their team and the business, no formal charts can help the project. It is important that people feel ownership of the overall project, rather than their own individual pieces.

I didn't delay it...

- Team members/sub teams not communicating effectively
- Team was not engaged enough to own the project
- 'My work- Your work'

- Added one more sheet to reporting/measurement
- Did not look at the intangibles like engagement, big picture?

C. *A senior leader told us this story in one of our very recent interactions with him. That when he had joined the telecom company as the head of a complex technology vertical, with a team of thirty professionals, he was perplexed to see that the team had been performing poorly against their KPIs (Key Performance Indicators). It was a central department responsible for guiding the regional teams towards the right solutions, resolving their issues as they emerged in real time and arranging the necessary approvals for the required capital expenditure.*

As they dealt in complex technology, the central team was organised into smaller vertical teams, each focusing on a narrow field of study. The turnaround time to resolve the issues by each of the vertical teams was very high, despite the fact that the team had the best technical expertise in the whole company. The regional teams were dissatisfied with the department and raised their concerns to the Chief Technology Officer. While digging deeper into the problem, he found multiple concerns around accountability, trust and cooperation within the team.

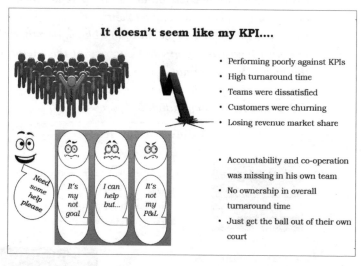

It doesn't seem like my KPI....

- Performing poorly against KPIs
- High turnaround time
- Teams were dissatisfied
- Customers were churning
- Losing revenue market share

- Accountability and co-operation was missing in his own team
- No ownership in overall turnaround time
- Just get the ball out of their own court

Usually, the regional team would make a request to one of the verticals for support, but the solution would need cooperation from other verticals too. However, instead of sitting together to resolve the issue, teams worked serially one after the other causing multiple iterations and resulting in delays. So, while the patient was dying, the teams were all busy proving that the other vertical team was the one that was standing on the oxygen pipe.

There was no ownership in the overall turnaround time, just the ownership to get the ball out of their court. The group showed all the symptoms of being disengaged and treating their work as just a job. They did not have a view of the big picture, and did not act as one team. They considered their closest colleagues as their biggest rivals.

Disengagement is the Root Cause

One might say that some of the issues highlighted in the previous chapter can be solved by setting the right processes and adhering to them, using the right techniques and proper workflows. And you would probably be right in case we lived in a static world.

Can we assume that processes once created will always remain optimal? Can we define methods for all scenarios? Do we hope that no new scenarios will emerge?

What happens when a process outlives its usefulness? If each person just limits themselves to his/her role in it, who will look for new solutions, techniques or methods? What if new cases start emerging and the existing processes cannot handle them? Will they fall through the cracks?

Processes, techniques and measures only become a bunch of redundant spreadsheets, charts and tools unless people bring them to life by using their heart and soul. The senior leaders need to understand that they are dealing with human beings and that leaders must ensure adequate engagement for their people. Human beings are not just driven by salaries or incentives alone, rather most of the time, they are motivated by softer aspects of the work environment such as trust, relationships, ownership etc. The onus for building the right environment is on the leaders. If an organisation has leaders who can engage people (not just their direct reports but whole teams), only then can we envisage any collaboration across teams.

Properly engaged teams never just focus on their role alone or just pre-established ways to conducting business. While they keep the end goal in mind, they adjust the course of action, stretch and think out of the box, collaborate and create new ways to meet the needs of the customer (internal or external) and ultimately support the success of the company.

With increased focus on innovation and an agile way of working, there is a trend in new age companies to do away with so called processes. Under such circumstances the importance of engagement grows even further.

What are Leaders Losing due to Disengaged Teams?

Engagement is no more a "nice to have" feature, rather it is a basic "essential" element, one that is non-negotiable. When there are disengaged teams, leaders and ultimately organisations are losing a lot. It is not only some money they are losing either in the form of extra costs or loss of profit, but they may also be losing the capability to keep the organisation ahead of the market and even alive or viable in the medium to long term.

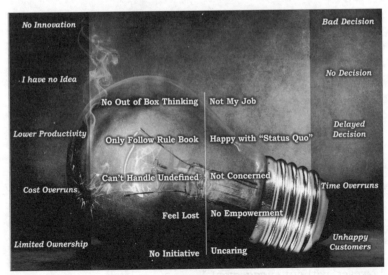

I Am Disengaged

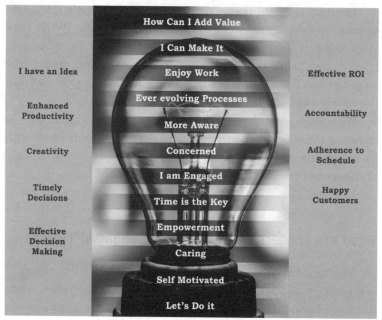

I Am Engaged

While working with some of the clients, we came across a few factors that affect a team's performance:

No Innovation

When teams are disengaged, they do not think about better ways of solving problems. They just do their bit, as an individual, and as per a defined process or instructions given to them. There cannot be any innovation, if new ways are not explored. The saying, if you always do what you've always done, you will always get what you've always got, rings true.

Engaged employees are the key to innovation. A Canadian Government Executive article very aptly states that, "there is no innovation without engagement. Innovation is the perfect storm of a great idea, motivated individuals and a culture of higher performance coming together to produce a meaningful improvement on the status quo. None of these things is possible, however, without engagement."[1]

Poor Ownership and Accountability

A disengaged team takes limited ownership of the overall success of the team. Typically, the focus is on what the employee is doing, and as long as they are doing a decent job, they are satisfied. Furthermore, the expectation is that the manager will tell them what to do, and at times even how to do the job. Telling the employees what to do makes the job of the manager demanding, tiring and at times frustrating. As explained by the timeless Harvard Business Review article, "Management Time: Who's got the Monkey"[2] the manager retains all the monkeys on her/his back and ends up doing all the work. A key to outstanding team performance requires people to be more accountable and responsible. Only engaged employees and teams develop a sense of ownership and accountability.

Hampered Productivity

Every company wants to be more productive. But it is easier said than done.

Only by using the principles of employee engagement, you can boost productivity in your organisation without adding substantially to costs. It is reported by the Gallup[3] that organisations with a higher level of employee engagement do report 22% higher productivity. Employees engaged with their job and company feel valued and are more productive as they are motivated beyond their personal needs or compliance. They are more focused, efficient and keep the company's success in mind.

Bad Customer Service

When an employee is disengaged, it starts reflecting in his/her behaviour and/or actions.

When engaging with a client, the initial response of such an employee is non-committal. Such employees claim powerlessness and pass the buck to an unseen management to make decisions. They reduce their own credibility and the customer's confidence in the company.

There is an interesting piece of work by Christine Fletcher 'How Employee Engagement Helps Drive Customer Experience'. She mentions, there is research showing that an engaged workforce is a key to a better customer experience. She further adds, "Your employees are an important piece of the customer-experience puzzle. It is impossible to have a seamless end-to-end brand experience if your employees do not have a customer-centric mindset and the motivation to keep customers happy."[4]

Delayed Decision-Making

When teams are disengaged, they feel less empowered. Disempowered teams are responsible for delayed decision-making. Delayed decisions lead to additional costs and/or lost opportunities.

W.M. Greenfield, in one of his articles, emphasises the importance of employee engagement in decision-making. Here are a few excerpts, "Making choices is something we all do naturally. Making sensible decisions, on the other hand, is an art and a process. One needs to want to do it... The pace of change in companies is accelerating. Decisions need to be made more rapidly. Often, the 'higher-ups' who once made all-important decisions are not available quickly enough or have insufficient time and information to make the required decisions. These changes in the structure of business decision-making thus makes it imperative that employees know how to make wise decisions and, more important, that management is confident that all employees will make the right decisions when called on to decide."[5]

All the above factors affect the company detrimentally in many ways including the following:

- Reduced revenues
- Added expenses
- Limited company growth
- Poor branding

The Impact in Numbers

The evidence of the importance of engagement within teams and corporations is overwhelming.

In some very recent surveys, it is reported that only 13% to 25% of the workforce feels engaged at work. This shocking result suggests that the rest of the employees are not engaged. These are alarming numbers!

Let us look at some of the implications that translate into costs to a company. Below are some references from research conducted over the past few years.

Reese Haydon of DescisionWise, an American management consulting company, has found some compelling correlations regarding how much disengaged employees can cost a company. One of the surveys mentioned that disengaged employee costs an organisation approximately $3,400 for every $10,000 in annual salary; a staggering 34% of lost productivity[6].

Keith Ayers, CEO of IntegroLeadership Institute, mentioned that, "In many companies, a lack of employee engagement costs the organisation anywhere between 35% to 50% of payroll, as employees do not give the organisation 100% of what they are capable."[7] In monetary terms, this means that a lack of engagement in a 100-person company with an annual salary cost of $5million costs the company anywhere from $1.75 million to $2.50 million on a yearly basis. A significant loss of value to the company.

Gallup Inc, a leading American research based, global performance management consulting company, have found some astonishing facts on the disengagement of managers and leaders. Gallup mentions in their survey that 51% of managers are not engaged, and a further 14% are actively disengaged. The article states "by Gallup's estimates, the 'not engaged' group costs the US, $77 billion to $96 billion annually through their impact on those they manage and when we factor in the impact of the 'actively disengaged' groups, those figures jump to $319 billion to $398 billion annually."

"It is further reported that employees who are supervised by highly engaged managers are 59% more likely to be engaged than those supervised by actively disengaged managers."[8]

If companies want to bolster productivity and profitability, increase customer loyalty, operating income and lower absenteeism; employees need to be engaged at all levels.

Warning Signs

So how do you know if the teams and people within the teams are disengaged? We found quite a few signs of disengaged teams, The diagram below shows some of the indicative ones. In case you notice even two signs out of these, you may safely assume that the team suffers from disengagement and that it is time for you to take action.

Warning Signs

Technology Leaders are Conditioned Differently

Working in technology domains such as planning, engineering, design, architecture, solutions, products, research and development, etc., conditions your mind to think in a certain way. This is natural and to be expected. Some friends who have been into technology for decades, knowingly or unknowingly see their personal lives also from a project plan's lens. What we are trying to say here is that we in technology get conditioned in a certain way over the years and our brains and styles are greatly influenced by this.

You were chosen to become a leader based on the expertise that you gained as a technologist. But, it is important to note that as Marshall Goldsmith said, "What got you here, will not get you there."[9] You may have to gain new expertise to become a better leader.

Somewhere among the complex skills that helped you become a Technology leader lies the key to the path forward. Listed below are some of the key skills that Technology leaders typically excel at.

Now is the time for you to build on your skills and become that truly great leader that you always wanted to be. This book is all about leveraging your skills to bridge any gaps.

Execution Focus

While you were in the process of becoming a leader, you were in fact working for one. The leader did most of the strategic thinking, breaking goals into tasks and milestones. Your success was measured by your ability to achieve these milestones and to show results with a single-minded focus. In the process, your focus was always on the next milestone or target to achieve and was limited to tactical work.

Since there was appreciation each time you achieved your milestones, and you are rewarded for these successes, the behaviour got reinforced so you tended to neglect the tasks that may not have provide immediate success. Tasks like nurturing teams, relationships, etc., were left for later and given less importance.

As a leader, while task execution is still an important skill, you will need to complement it with other leadership skills such as engaging your people.

Tech Minded, Not Leadership Minded

You were the master of details, details that your leader felt comfortable in delegating completely to you, depending solely on your expertise. The more you demonstrated this expertise, the more confident your leader became in you.

Again, your success reinforced this into a behaviour that made you more technology-oriented and not really leadership-oriented; focusing on more technical, more detail-oriented tasks while neglecting or giving less importance to the softer aspects of the job/role.

Like the execution skill, technology orientation is a great skill but as a leader you will have to complement it with leadership orientation.

Tangible, Measurable Parameters versus Intangibility of Human Behaviour

Directing came easily to you, defining tasks by numbers, that could be measured and the ones that had a tangible impact on the progress. You could define steps and guide team members to do a perfect job. Developing team members would take time and effort and mostly had an intangible value. You may have cared less about behaviours and feelings as long as the deliverables were taken care of. The people in your team had much lesser impact on the overall scheme of things and hence the intangible impact of their behaviours may not have really been your focus; their delivery was. However, as a leader, employee development also becomes a natural extension for great performance.

Deadlines and Deliveries

"What" and "When" dominated your days. Milestones, goals, tasks, resources, planning, execution, dates and timelines; these dictated your every working moment. You were the best person for the job. "Deliver on time, every time" that may have been your mantra. "How" was not that important, you dealt with problems in real time and your capability to overcome them defined success. Investing time in activities that were not related to immediate deliverables may have seemed to be a waste of time. As a leader, you will have to focus on "How" as well in addition to "What" and "When".

Thus, the recipe for being an effective leader includes new skills such as employee engagement and development.

A Leader Must Engage Her/His Team to be Effective, but What is "Engagement"?

All leaders want to lead teams effectively; they want to engage and mobilise their team to gain greater results for themselves and their organisation. However, it appears that many do not know where to start. Engagement is a word that has been used in the corporate world for quite some time now. Yet, its meaning can vary depending on the company and its environment. Some people think engagement is taking teams to lunches and parties; some think team building events constitute engagement. Thus, it can become overwhelming and at times confusing for leaders to understand and know what to do to create and maintain an engaged team. Some believe it is HR's job to do it and others feel it is the organisation's responsibility. Often HR sends out reports on engagement, which most of the leaders do not understand, nor can relate to and find it all too difficult.

What Exactly is Engagement Then?

Engagement in simple words, is when each of your team members is willingly putting the extra effort required to meet the end goal, when teams are aligned to the bigger purpose, always motivated enough to take on challenges, when boundaries do not limit them from making a customer happy, when they feel empowered to make the decisions on behalf of the company and most importantly, they have confidence in your support when they take risks to make "magic" happen.

References

1. Chavremootoo, Belinda. *"There Is No Innovation without Engagement."* Canadian Government Executive, Canadian Government Executive, 13 May 2014, canadiangovernmentexecutive.ca/there-is-no-innovation-without-engagement/

2. Wass, William OnckenJr.Donald L., et al. *"Management Time: Who's Got the Monkey?"* Harvard Business Review, Harvard Business Review, 18 July 2017, hbr.org/1999/11/management-time-whos-got-the-monkey

3. Baldoni, John. *"Employee Engagement Does More than Boost Productivity."* Harvard Business Review, Harvard Business Review, 7 Aug. 2014, hbr.org/2013/07/employee-engagement-does-more

4. Fletcher, Christine. *"How Employee Engagement Helps Drive Customer Experience."* Vision Critical, Vision Critical, 24 June 2016, www.visioncritical.com/employee-engagement-drives-customer-experience/

5. Greenfield, W. M. *"Decision Making and Employee Engagement."* Employment Relations Today, Wiley Subscription Services, Inc., A Wiley Company, 8 July 2004, onlinelibrary.wiley.com/doi/10.1002/ert.20013/pdf

6. Haydon, Reese. *"Show Me the Money: The ROI of Employee Engagement."* DecisionWise, 27 Dec. 2016, www.decision-wise.com/show-me-the-money-the-roi-of-employee-engagement/

7. Ayers, Keith E. *"Keith Ayers - Engagement Is Not Enough."* Keith Ayers - Engagement Is Not Enough, Keith Ayers, 2008, www.engagementisnotenough.com/

8. Gallup, Inc. *"Only 35% of U.S. Managers Are Engaged in Their Jobs."* Gallup.com, Gallup News, 2 Apr. 2015, news.gallup.com/businessjournal/182228/managers-engaged-jobs.aspx

9. Goldsmith, Marshall, and Reiter, Mark. *What Got You Here Won't Get You There: How Successful People Become Even More Successful!* Hyperion, 2014

Introduction to HUMAN

Based on our collective experiences as leaders and coaches for technology organisations, we have designed the HUMAN framework especially for leaders in technology organisations. It is simple, easy to understand and execute, yet extremely effective for engaging teams.

Let's have a look at the framework.

H	**Heeding** to your basic characteristics of being a leader. It is about a leader being aware of his/her own self.
U	**Understanding** team members, their roles and their alignment to the big picture and vision.
M	**Messaging** – Sending right messages, sharing stories and feedback.
A	**Acknowledging** – Acknowledgement and rewards.
N	**Nurturing** team members to be better leaders and enable them to do their best.

The HUMAN framework is a no-fluff way to help you engage and mobilise your teams when you work for a technology organisation, or if you have been a technologist yourself. This framework works elegantly to take out, to a large extent, the subjectivity and brings in the objectivity and measures around this critical area. HUMAN is a foolproof methodology, which lays down a step-by-step process to take care of your people engagement needs.

HUMAN starts with helping you to become aware of yourself, starting from within and looking at some fundamental traits such as your trustworthiness, competence, resilience etc. The idea is to enable you to see things from your own perspective. Once you become more aware of yourself, the framework helps you to understand each of the team members and then helps you start taking small steps to engage your team members more effectively at work. This framework is helpful for leaders who have a maximum of ten to twelve direct reports. There may be further teams under your direct reports and the total team size could well be in tens or several hundreds.

Each of the letters of HUMAN is an element to support effective engagement for your team.

When you first start working with the framework, it is suggested that you work on one element, practice it for some time and be familiar with it before moving onto the next element. However, once you are through all the elements, they will work together i.e. simultaneously and this framework will become your new norm.

Let us explain briefly what each element entails.

H (Heeding Yourself)

This element of the framework helps you in "Heeding Yourself", explore a bit more about yourself, and recognise where you are, and where you want to reach with regard to your feelings, behaviour and attitude. To understand yourself, you need to be truthful and honest with yourself. "H" is the beginning of a journey of self-exploration and discovery.

There are generally three images associated with self; the first one is the Real Self, second one is the one that is based on wishful thinking, this one we call Imagined Self and the third one, which is based on others' perception of you, which is based on your interactions with them, we call this the Perceived Self. Imagined Self is based on your expectations of self. So how do you know what is Real Self? What if you start working on making the Perceived Self as close to the Imagined Self? You will be easily able to deduce that in such a case, Imagined Self = Perceived Self = Real Self. The idea behind H is to start being aware of the gaps between the Perceived Self and the Imagined Self.

Once you have analysed yourself and as a consequence become more self-aware, you can start bridging those gaps to meet your expectations of Imagined Self. Bridging those gaps help gain a more fulfilling relationship with yourselves and in turn others.

U (Understanding)

Now, once you understand more about yourself, it is time to know more about your team members. Once you become self-aware, your perception and ability to know others will be different. You may say, I already understand my team members, which is an encouraging start.

But do keep in mind that whatever you may know is about your perception of them and that a similar gap exists between your perception of them and their expectations of self. This exercise is an attempt to bridge this gap. You will end up knowing more about the team members and this will help in clarifying a lot of gaps. A lot also depends on how you go about collecting the information that creates your perception. Currently it may be based on some specific interactions and may be limited and subjective.

But the feeling will be entirely different when you look at understanding your team members in a more objective way. This will ultimately help you become more connected and successful.

This element of the framework will enable you to have objective discussions for creating a mutually agreed understanding with your team members. The process will be quite simple and straightforward and will enable you in more ways than one.

M (Messaging)

Once you know yourself, know your team members; other things start to become easier. The next element is how you communicate with your team, and how you plan and send the messages. Messages connect the team with you. Messages need to be tailored based on your understanding of the individual, so this builds upon the previous elements.

Messages are used for conveying strategy, plans, results, and sharing and receiving feedback. Messages can be delivered individually or to the team. Messaging can be written, verbal, non-verbal, etc. This part of the framework is all about strategizing your communication for the best effect. Delivering the right messages at the right time and in the right format and setting, adds to the effectiveness.

This part of the HUMAN framework will help you build an effective strategy around messaging.

A (Acknowledging)

All of us know that being acknowledged has a significant positive impact on us. It helps our motivation tremendously if somebody acknowledges our efforts and performance, and rewards us in the right way. While acknowledging may come naturally to some of us for others it may not. It may also depend on factors other than individual traits, for example, culture. While in some cultures it may be a norm to acknowledge, and appreciate, it is not necessarily universal.

We may also observe that different team members may have different reactions to an acknowledgement, while some may thank you, others may just claim that it was all because of you, some others may just not know how to handle it, some others may not accept it as they were just doing their job and may not consider themselves worthy of it.

How would you know whether your efforts at Acknowledging are moving in the right direction? For example, if you praise one of your team members too often for good work, you may end up alienating that member from all others, as the team may think of you as practicing favouritism. Are you doing a favour to the team member by praising him or subjecting him to punishment? Will it lead to better engagement or worsen it?

Therefore, you will also need to think about the "How" part of acknowledgement in addition to the "Why" and "What".

This element demystifies all such issues and will help you to plan the acknowledgements and rewards for your team members in the best way. This systematic technique will help you overcome your limitations, if any, and make you better at encouraging and motivating the team.

N (Nurturing)

Once the primary aspects are set up, it is time to plan how to develop your team's skills and make them more efficient, productive and successful in their current role; as well as helping them develop for future opportunities. It requires a mindset shift when leaders not only think about their own development; they start thinking and working towards the development of their teams.

While all of the elements of HUMAN, will help you grow, get better results and respect from your team, your peers and management, the Nurturing element if executed properly, is the one that will get you the most respect from your team and will yield the most results in the longer term. As discussed early in the book, the more you work for your team, develop their skills, and empower them to do the job, the more time you will have to work on your own growth and development.

Like other elements, you will have to change your ways of working to be able to execute well on Nurturing. You may currently take pride in doing a good job of guiding your team and getting the best out of them, while the approach that you must take in Nurturing is about making your team more enabled and that they will be more independent over time in terms of delivering their work.

Nurturing your team will eventually yield extra time for yourself. You will have to also learn to invest the extra time for your own development. This development effort is the one that will yield more results for your own growth. In fact, you will now be responsible for finding growth for everyone in your team including yourself.

This is again a paradigm shift and this element of the framework helps you plan for the development requirements of your team in a systematic way and help you overcome any mindset challenges. In fact, you can use the tool for your own development planning as well.

Pre-Requisites for Applying HUMAN Framework

The primary requirement for applying this framework is a curiosity, a readiness to learn and willingness to invest time in developing your leadership knowledge and skills. In short, a desire to be the leader that you want to be. You will need to have the discipline to explore and try new things, unlearn things that do not serve you well, replacing them with new learning, have the ability to receive feedback and be able to reflect on your leadership journey making positive and lasting changes. Be prepared that most of the elements may present a new paradigm and could be potentially challenging to begin with. Trust in yourself, and the framework as well as consistency in execution will help you overcome the hurdles that may come your way.

One of the suggestions that we have for you to become successful in using this framework is to have a peer/friend who is privy to this journey of yours and with whom you can regularly sit and review your progress. He/she should be the one you can have complete confidence in, and the one who can push you to be honest with yourself. This will help you achieve the transformation in a time bound manner.

How Will It Work?

Each element of the framework is explained in the following chapters.

Every component of the framework is further elaborated using a story of the journey of a leader, Arun, who is struggling to engage his team. Although this story is a piece of fiction, it simulates scenarios from a technology organisation.

The story mentioned is only from a perspective of creating a better understanding of the framework. Though the story happens to be setup in a specific type of software development organisation, this framework is meant to be used in any technology organisation.

It may also be relevant to mention here that the HUMAN framework is designed to work for all leadership levels and styles, as all leaders can benefit by engaging their team better.

Also in the story the protagonist Arun, is facing a challenge and needs to take steps to improve his team performance. In a way, his hand is forced. He learns to be a great leader, because he has no other choice. Let us use his story to learn but also make sure, that we do not wait too long to learn to be a good leader that our hand also gets forced.

Action Time

Worksheets called "Action Time" have been provided for facilitating learning as part of the HUMAN framework. For each element of "Action Time" a detailed explanation has also been provided. The "Action Time" is designed to help you make steady progress on your journey.

We encourage you to setup the following mechanisms for the purpose of the recording and checking your progress as you complete various exercises listed through this framework:

- Maintain the record of all "Action Time" documents that you create.

- Maintain the course of action that you decide, following each exercise.

- Setup a review process, either a self-review or review with a peer/friend as suggested earlier.

- Maintain a record of your observations about any noticeable change in yourself or in your team members.

If you wish, you could maintain a personal journal to record your observations, experiences etc. in the form of a notebook or as a softcopy, whatever is more convenient. A personal journal also known as diary or a log, is commonly defined as a written record of incidents, experiences, and ideas.

Story Play

This part provides the context of the story and an introduction to the characters. Every component of the HUMAN framework is elaborated using a story of the journey of a leader, Arun, who is struggling to engage his team. The organisation chart below is a partial chart that highlights the position of Arun, our protagonist in the organisation hierarchy. For the purpose of simplicity we have only shown the direct reports for Arun. Though each of his direct reports has his own team, they are not covered in this story. The context of the story is an offshore software development centre.

It is a product development organisation which is working in alignment with their on-site team. The on-site team is responsible for the end client management. The on-site team takes the actual requirements and passes it on to their off-shore development centre. In this context, the on-site team becomes a client to the off-shore team.

Anupam's role, as Head of Offshore Development, is to get quality deliverables to his customers and generate more business from his on-site team. The way to achieve this is through his teams delivering quality products/services, within the agreed timeline and budget. Anupam has a good reputation with his on-site team, and he is always deeply concerned about keeping this reputation. He does not want it to be spoilt and is very careful about all the deliverables that go out. He relies heavily on the feedback from this on-site team about his teams and their delivery.

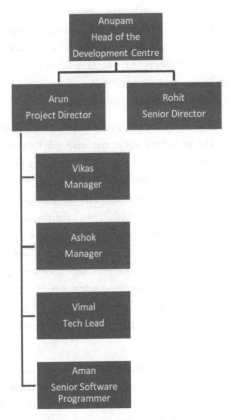

Characters in the story

Arun is our Project Director, and the leader we will be following in this story. He joined this organisation four months ago and has been assigned to a new project just three months back. He reports directly to Anupam. Arun has extensive experience in the business as a project manager and has so far managed only small projects. His most recent project was successful through his hard work and his personal drive to deliver. This current project, which he has been leading for the past three months, is much bigger in scope, with many more people reporting to him. He knows that this project is crucial for the organisation and that failing to deliver would not help his career. Furthermore, he feels outside his comfort zone, leading a larger group of people. So far, his relationship with his team has been only transactional in nature. Arun is not confident about building relationships. He also does not easily recognise or accept his challenge areas. Taking feedback is hard for him as he always becomes defensive. Many of his direct reports are also senior people with similar years of experience, and at times, Arun feels somewhat inferior and feels that he is in competition with them.

Vikas is a Senior Software Programmer and a team manager in the project. He is responsible for one part of the project. His management style is a mix of authoritative and consultative. He wants the best results but would like his team to always listen to him. He has been in the organisation for the past four months, and this is his first project with this company. He knows and feels that his experience and his immediate manager Arun's experience level is almost the same. In the past three months since the start of the project, he has faced ego issues with Arun, and he has been unhappy working with Arun. He talks to people outside the team about the shortcomings of his manager. He and Arun do not get along with each other. For Arun, Vikas is a difficult person to manage.

Ashok is a Senior Software Programmer and another team manager in the project. He wants to be in everyone's good books. He has been with the organisation for more than a year. He is good at technology and has a curiosity to learn new technologies. He is an introvert, avoids conflict and does not open up much with his colleagues. His way of working is mostly hierarchical, i.e. he shares the relevant information only if he feels that the person in front has authority. He chooses not to share information, knowledge or learning with his team, colleagues and manager unless it has to be shared. He thinks he knows the right way to do things and does not communicate effectively. He pretends to listen to people, but always has the last word. He does not share a great rapport with Arun but openly does not say anything.

Vimal is a hardcore techie and the Technical Lead. He loves coding. He wants to be left alone to do his job and wants everybody to recognise him as a great technical resource. He is super enthusiastic and an excited young man. Arun does not match his enthusiasm and finds it challenging to talk to him. Vimal keeps asking Arun repeatedly for more challenging work because he needs the stimulus to remain focused and interested in the project.

Aman is a Senior Software Programmer in Arun's team. He is an experienced programmer and has worked in this role for many years. But work does not interest him much. He works only to be able to sustain a living and provide for his family. The recent project assigned to him is almost the same as before. The only difference is that he has been recently promoted to a team lead role and Arun is his new project director.

Rohit is a Senior Director who is responsible for various client engagements. While he is delivery-oriented, he is also known as a people's person. He has built a strong reputation for not only delivering quality work but also being able to create a trusting relationship with his own teams, and with various other teams across the business. Rohit's has an amazing ability to take everybody along with him, with or without authority. He is not directly responsible for this project.

The project has an on-site team; this team is Arun's client. The on-site team shares the end customer's requirements with Arun's team. The on-site team is directly responsible to the end customer. As mentioned above, Anupam, the head of off-shore development centre, has a great relationship with the on-site team, so it is essential that Arun and his team have a good relationship and understanding of the on-site counterparts to deliver a successful project.

Day 0: A Call to Action

As mentioned above, Arun is three months into the project, and is currently managing the early development phase of the product. Arun gets the feedback from Anupam that his team is not performing well. Anupam shares with Arun that he is constantly getting not so positive feedback from on-site team. That the initial deliverables have been delayed and the quality of the deliverables has been reported as poor. It is hard for Arun to absorb this feedback and he feels that it is the early stages of the project and that he has not yet had a chance to perform.

Anupam provides additional feedback telling Arun that he believes that Arun does not have a satisfactory relationship with his team and that this needs to change if Arun is going to be successful. Anupam also informs Arun that the on-site team does not have much confidence in him. Arun tries to explain the circumstances to Anupam. After listening for a while, Anupam tells Arun that things are not going to work unless he has good relationship with his team and the on-site team. He tells Arun that unlike the previous projects that Arun has handled, this project is much larger in scale and requires the whole team to work together to make it a success. He is expecting Arun to bring the team together and lead them to success.

He shares that the on-site team is getting inconsistent messages from his team managers. It appears that his team does not seem to be in sync with each other. He conveys that it is expected that as a good leader he engages with his team and leads them to making the project a success. Anupam warns him that if it continues to be like this, the project will be taken over by somebody else. Anupam makes it very clear to Arun that it is an important project for the organisation and he cannot take any chances with this one.

What Has Good Relationship Got to Do with It ?

Arun leaves the meeting feeling very despondent; he has been working very hard to get quality deliverables; working late nights with team members, telling them what they need to do, etc. He is not sure that having a good relationship with his team members is so important. He believes that in order to have a cordial relationship, he will have to socialise with them. He believes he is not ready to do that. He and everyone else just need to get the job done. Arun leaves wondering how best he can tackle this issue. Can he actually fix it? Should he be looking for another job?

Day 1: A Call for Help

The next day after a restless night at home and hours of reflecting, Arun decides to talk to his close friend, and a senior colleague Rohit. Rohit is undoubtedly successful. Rohit has been working with the organisation for the past two years. They have known each other for many years and in fact, he is the one who introduced Arun to the hiring team for this role. Arun feels that if he could be half as competent as Rohit, then he would still be a much better leader.

Arun invites Rohit for coffee, to catch up. Arun explains his situation to Rohit and seeks his support. Rohit listens to Arun's concerns and the whole episode with Anupam.

Rohit: How are you feeling about the whole situation?

Arun: I am feeling lost. I have worked hard but just not able to manage the tantrums of my team members. I am feeling as if Anupam has given me a warning that I may lose my job, in case I do not fix things. And I do not understand anything about the "good relationship" angle.

Rohit: What is it you would like to do now?

Arun: See, I don't know. Anupam told me in one way or the other that I am not a good leader. My team is not in sync. I am not able to manage my team and relationship with the on-site team. I don't know what to do.

Rohit: Take a deep breath and tell me frankly how much you agree with what Anupam said?

Arun: Frankly, I think he is right to an extent. I have handled smaller teams earlier and relatively junior people. I have never handled a big team and people with such knowledge and experience. It seems he is expecting me to have a good relationship and deliver the good results at the same time. I believe either I can work or make relationships. Where is the time for both? And even if I make good relationships, how will it help improve product quality or team coordination?

Rohit: That is a great point. How do you think you can work or get the work done if you don't have a good rapport with the team?

Arun: What do you think?

Rohit: In my experience, you must have a rapport with the team. You need to spend time to build a good understanding. It is your responsibility to engage your team members in a way that they are all aligned to what the whole team is supposed to deliver. With bigger roles, delivering successfully starts becoming a complex task with many variables. Simple project management skills may not work. You will need to work on creating alignment and co-ordination within your larger team as well as related functions. Engaging your team in an effective manner is a key to business success.

Arun: Wow, it sounds good, but is it possible to do that? I mean, I know you are a great leader. People appreciate you as a people's leader. But from where I am right now, do you think it is possible for me?

Rohit: Of course! But how important is it for you?

Arun: It is important, very important indeed. You know this project is critical and I need my team to perform at their best and help me deliver this one successfully. I came to this organisation with an expectation that I can successfully handle the bigger role and this project. In case this project is not a success, it will become a problem for my whole career. But even if I want to engage my team in a better way, I don't know where to start.

Rohit is happy about this answer and tells Arun that he is very happy to know that he has a desire to make this change. He comments that Arun has been very successful as a project manager so far and that has helped him to get to his current role. Anupam must have confidence in Arun's abilities as he has made him the leader for one of the most important projects. Also, he appreciated that Anupam took time to understand the situation and that he shared his concerns openly with Arun. Rohit is happy that Anupam has also given Arun guidance in terms of "working on his team", which again illustrates that Anupam is quite confident of Arun's technical and project management skills, but wants him to develop another aspect of leadership.

Rohit tells Arun that the path forward will be different and as Arun may not be familiar with it, it may look difficult or obscure. He gives confidence to Arun that he himself has gone through this journey and has used a simple framework which will make it very easy for Arun to negotiate this new territory. He also tells Arun that the framework that he is suggesting will leverage quite a few of the skills that made Arun successful so far and have helped him to become a leader for a large and important project.

He tells Arun that the framework he is suggesting is called HUMAN. He has used it himself and this very framework has helped him on his journey to becoming a successful leader. It has helped him devise various ways to engage his teams in a satisfying way.

Arun is curious and expresses a desire to learn more about this framework.

What Next?

Subsequent chapters explain about each element of the HUMAN framework in detail.

All the chapters also share Arun's journey of discovery on how to effectively engage his team. Each chapter shares the relevant discussions between Arun and Rohit, as well as examples of the filled exercises by Arun. Chapters also cover all common dilemmas that a leader may have and offer clarity in terms of the information shared by Rohit with Arun as part of the dialogues as well as Arun's own reflections as he progresses through the framework.

We are sure that you will find Arun's journey interesting and that you too will be able to gain from this framework!

Are you ready to start?

Let's go!

H

Heeding
Yourself

*"Many leadership problems are
driven by low self-awareness."*

-Bill Hybels

H – Heeding Yourself

The HUMAN framework believes that engagement starts with the self.

As discussed earlier in the book, the idea behind "H" is to start being aware of the gaps between the Perceived Self and the Imagined Self. The idea is to heed your Real Self, i.e., to be aware of your strengths, challenges, behaviours etc.

If you are not aware of your strengths, challenges and behaviours and their impact on others, you will not be able to engage the people around yourself satisfactorily. In fact, your efforts to engage the team will end up producing mixed results and it may leave you more confused about what really works.

The "H" element of the HUMAN framework provides a systematic way to explore about yourself, discover the gaps as well as create a plan to overcome these gaps.

You will start by reflecting and answering a few questions about yourself. You need to begin to explore more about yourself. In doing so, you need to be honest, truly honest.

You are encouraged to answer the questions from not only your point of view but more importantly from your immediate team members' standpoint. You are also encouraged to have formal or informal discussions with your team members with an aim to get their feedback. The more honest you are while doing this exercise, the more awareness it will create within you.

At the same time, if you are not comfortable seeking feedback, you can choose to record your own point of view to start with. As this is a living document, you will always have the opportunity to seek feedback at a later date and incorporate modifications to your plan accordingly.

Once you are through identifying your own opinion and that of your team members, the next step is to identify the main behaviours that can contribute towards betterment of the identified attributes.

Apart from the time required for feedback, it is advised to set aside some 30-45 minutes for this initial exercise.

Take a couple of deep breaths and reflect upon the following attributes. It is suggested to think of at least two examples where you have exhibited the particular attribute. It will help you to reflect deeper and be surer and authentic about the answer you are going to record.

Action Time: Heeding Yourself
Know Yourself

Attribute	My View	Feedback (Consolidated)	Behaviour for Betterment
Competence			
Trust			

Attribute	My View	Feedback (Consolidated)	Behaviour for Betterment
Commitment to role			
Integrity			
Resilience			

Attribute	My View	Feedback (Consolidated)	Behaviour for Betterment
Do I serve?			
Caring			
Commitment to team members success?			

Attribute	My View	Feedback (Consolidated)	Behaviour for Betterment
Admitting mistakes			
Lead by example			
Respect			

Attribute	My View	Feedback (Consolidated)	Behaviour for Betterment
Say – Do ratio			

What are the other behaviours that may help me be a better leader?

You should write the answers in the above "Action Time". These answers will help you know more about yourself and help you be able to identify gaps between the Perceived Self and your Imagined Self.

The table below provides you with explanation for each of the element above and also provides you with some of the leading questions that you might use to understand more about yourself and to seek feedback from your team members.

DESCRIPTION Action Time: Heeding Yourself Know Yourself			
Attribute	**My View**	**Feedback (Consolidated)**	**Behaviours for Betterment**
Competence	Do I know my subject as required by my role? How competent am I? What are the gaps, how can I fill them?	What do you think about my subject knowledge?	Identify behaviours that will help you better demonstrate the relevant attribute.
Trust	How trustworthy am I? Do my team members confide in me? Am I the first one, they will share a problem with?	What encourages or prevents you from sharing problems with me? What do you want to see in a leader for you to trust him/her?	
Commitment to role	Do I demonstrate commitment through action? How Committed am I to my role?	Am I perceived as committed to the project at hand?	

Integrity	Do I demonstrate integrity through action?	Am I perceived as honest and fair?
Resilience	Do I sustain against challenges? When there is a problem, do I remain focused? How resilient am I?	Do I keep the team on track despite challenges? Do I come across as a resilient leader?
Do I serve?	Am I available when team members need help? Would my team members and others feel that I am looking after their interests and the business interests?	Am I available when you need help? Do you feel that I am looking after your interests and the business interests?
Caring	How much I care about my team?	How caring I come across as a leader?
Commitment to team members success?	Do I care about my team members success?	How committed I seem for your success?
Admitting mistakes	How often do I admit mistakes?	How often do I admit mistakes?
Lead by example	How often do I lead by example?	How often do I lead by example?

Respect	Do I seek respect? Do I respect others?	Do you feel that I respect you?	
Say – Do ratio	Do my words and actions match?	Do my words and actions match?	

What are the other behaviours that may help me be a better leader?

(While thinking about other attributes, please do note down any other behaviour that you may identify as important for making you a better leader.)

The questions are designed to be simple and relatively easy to understand, all you need to do now is to honestly respond to these questions. As said before, you are encouraged to answer the questions from your own point of view and your immediate team member's viewpoint. You can reflect upon interactions that you had with them over past few months. For feedback, you may consider having formal or informal discussions with your team members.

After answering the above questions, you will have a set of key behaviours that can help you perform better. While there may be multiple behaviours that may emerge as important, our suggestion is that you should work on a behaviour at a time. Once you have achieved desired results for a behaviour, you can begin working on the second and so on.

Please select one behaviour that you feel is the most important to you right now, which is going to help you become the leader that you want to be.

Once you have identified the behaviour you need to work on, think about:

- What is that you want to change?
- How are you going to do that?
- What difference will people specifically see in you?

- How are you going to get the feedback?

It is important to get feedback so you know that you are doing the right thing and doing what you need to do, to be more effective.

Do not commit to more than one behaviour change at one point in time. Focus on that one aspect that will have the greatest positive impact on you as a leader. You will continue to focus on yourself as you continue to go through the process of using the framework HUMAN.

Below is a template to help you track your progress on the behaviour. The template is in two parts, part one is about helping you to plan the behaviour change journey and part two is about recording your progress as you continue your journey. Please use this template to keep a record. It is fun and encouraging to look back and see how far you have come. Writing it down helps you to reflect. All the great leaders reflect, that is one of the things that makes them great.

Action Time: Heeding Yourself Behaviour Change Journey	
Make a note of the behaviour that you want to change.	
How will I demonstrate this behaviour at work? What will be seen and heard?	
With the changed behaviour– How will I feel? How will others feel?	
What opportunities do I have at work to demonstrate this behaviour?	
Accountability partner – Who will help to keep me on track? (Don't hesitate to ask for help/guidance)	
Feedback – Who can provide me with feedback?	

Provided below is a format for journal entries that can be used to track the progress on the Behaviour Change Journey.

Action Time: Heeding Yourself Behaviour Change Journal			
Parameter	**Day 01**	**Day 07**	**Day 15**
Impact on my work How has this change in behaviour impacted my work?			
Impact on my team How has this change in behaviour impacted my team?			
Impact on my work satisfaction How has this change in behaviour impacted my work satisfaction?			

83

Feedback			
Parameter	**Day 01**	**Day 07**	**Day 15**
What feedback have I received?			
Who provided me the feedback?			

Let us understand more about each parameter of the "Action Time" above.

DESCRIPTION Action Time: Heeding Yourself Behaviour Change Journey	
Parameter	**Description**
Make a note of the behaviour that you want to change.	Note down details about the behaviour that you would like to change. What is it that you want to do? It could be as simple as listening ability or punctuality as long as you decide that it will have a positive impact on yourself and your team.

How will I demonstrate this behaviour at work? What will be seen and heard?	It contains your view on how you will demonstrate the right behaviour. In other words, what are the things which you do or say differently? It is about how and what you will do differently. You cannot control other people's behaviour, so you have to think about what best you can do in your current environment with current set of people, limitations and challenges.
With the changed behaviour– How will I feel? How will others feel?	The change in behaviour may bring changes in your feelings as well as that of others, during your interactions with them. Please make a note of your own feelings. Also, please note the feelings others might be experiencing. It will be great if you can identify any changes compared to the previous interactions.
What opportunities do I have at work to demonstrate this behaviour?	What are the immediate opportunities where you can show your new behaviour? It could be meetings, conferences, feedback sessions, presentations or any other interaction. People may or may not notice the change in you immediately. The idea is to identify opportunities to practice the new behaviour, which is the most important step at this point of time.
Accountability partner – Who will help to keep me on track?	Who can hold you accountable, keep you on track? You should ideally choose an accountability partner to help you in the behaviour change process. Human behaviour is not easy to change. The accountability partner could be your colleague or spouse or parent or manager or friend etc. The accountability partner has the right to ask questions about your progress and you should be very honest with him/her. It is not mandatory to have a partner from your workplace. It is one person with whom you are comfortable talking to about this. Don't hesitate to ask for help and support, whenever it is needed.

Feedback – Who can provide me feedback?	Since it is a behaviour at work, you will need feedback from people at work. These will be people who are immediate stakeholders and are affected by your behaviour. You can choose two to four individuals who can provide you feedback. Taking feedback may not be an easy task but believe us, once you let go of your hesitation and ask for feedback, you feel better because you start to see results. The by-product of accepting the feedback is that people feel valued, they respect you more, and you end up having a more cordial relationship. It may be difficult for you to go and ask people for feedback but you must accept that others' feedback does matter. It will help you in many ways. There is no shame in telling your peer or subordinates or colleagues that you want to change something in yourself and seek feedback on the progress. Just going and asking somebody for a feedback itself is a huge transformational experience.

A brief explanation of the journal entries is as below:

DESCRIPTION

Action Time: Heeding Yourself

Behaviour Change Journal

You will need to consciously notice what is happening at the workplace as you are working on changing this behaviour and reflect on the following.

Parameter	Description
Impact on my work How has this change in behaviour impacted my work?	Write down if you have noticed any changes at work as a result of working on the behaviour. Plan to do this regularly. Do not feel bad if you don't notice an immediate impact. Keep working on it; you will certainly see results.

Impact on my team How has this change in behaviour impacted my team?	Mention what impact you have noticed in your team with the changes. How are they responding to you?
Impact on my work satisfaction How has this change in behaviour impacted my work satisfaction? .	Mention if there is any impact on your work satisfaction levels. You do not need any scientific measures for knowing the impact here. Please do write whatever you feel.
Feedback	
What feedback have I received?	Mention the feedback that you received.
Who provided me with the feedback?	Also, write the names of people who provided the feedback. You can keep following up with them as you continue your journey. Please do not forget to say thanks to the person who has provided the feedback.

The above exercise is to make you more aware of yourself. It enables you to look beyond the technical aspects and provides you with the capability and tools to reflect on your behaviours.

Doing the above exercise will start helping you to be more conscious of your behaviour supporting you to change. At times not seeing tangible results can be discouraging. Please do not worry and keep going.

Any behaviour change takes time, sometimes months. Keep maintaining the behaviour change journal, this will provide you with focus and discipline. You have to regularly update your journal entries. Choose a day of the week and schedule this in your calendar and update the journal with your observations every week for the first ninety days and then complete it up, every fifteen days. Maintain this journal for at least six months.

Congratulate yourself as you are taking the first step on your transformational journey.

Believing in yourself and the process will make you feel more equipped for this transformation.

Being More Aware

How Competent ?

Credible?

Resilient?

Accountable?

Do People Trust Me?

What Behaviours Do I Want to Change?

Who Can Give Me Feedback?

Heeding yourself

Here are some tips to consider:

Say Less of...	Say More of...
I am stuck...	I will do this one...
Never thought so...	Yes, good idea...
I do not need to change...	I am open to learn new things...

Do Less of	Do More of
Procrastination	Being a go-getter
Being in Denial	Being open to accept

Day 5: The story continues

At the next meeting, Rohit presents the first element of the HUMAN engagement framework. As Rohit explains, it feels like a herculean task to Arun. With all the mess, the stress and tensions around the project, his team and Anupam's perception about him, how will he find time to do this?

Rohit: How are you feeling, Arun?

Arun: Overwhelmed, how will I manage to do this?

Rohit: Arun, as a leader working with large teams, we need to maintain the focus on being objective. Right now, there is a mess and things are complicated and almost everything is subjective - he said, she said, a blame game and finger pointing. Many times, you will find that you do not know what is right and what is wrong?

Arun: How can I be objective under all this pressure?

Rohit: In this scenario, using the HUMAN framework helps bring more objectivity, and by going through the stages, things will become much clearer. Since most of us technical people love objectivity, we are usually happier when we see things in an open fashion. The HUMAN framework is especially tailored for people like us. Once you start to follow the framework, it will be much easier for you.

Arun: Okay, that seems good.

Rohit: You will start developing a different bond with yourself and getting the results would be much easier than in the current situation.

This discussion with Rohit gives him some hope as he really wants to improve his leadership competencies. Arun knows that the project is crucial not only to the organisation but also for his own career. However, he is still apprehensive about being unsuccessful and there exists a fear of being exposed through such an exercise.

Rohit can see this in Arun's body language and asks Arun, "What are your fears?"

Arun: I confess that I am afraid. It seems quite complicated and time consuming. Time is something that I do not have with the project deliverables already lagging behind schedule.

Rohit: What other apprehensions do you have?

Arun: Furthermore, how can I answer some of these questions about myself, I am afraid I have never done this before. I don't know if I am caring or if my team trusts me. How would I know this?

Rohit empathises with him and plans to spend some more time, reminding and discussing with Arun, how important this leadership transformation is for him at this point in his career. He reminds him of the feedback from Anupam. Arun has to put in concerted efforts to change the situation if he wants to be successful. Rohit mentions that this exercise is not going to be formally documented in his office records and that it is only for himself. It is an opportunity for him to explore and reach another level of leadership without any risks. He adds that it brings a lot of awareness of self and that being self-aware is the first step to becoming the leader you want to be.

He also explains that there are no right or wrong answers. Arun needs to reflect on the various attributes from his own point of view and his team's point of view, and record the facts honestly. This is where feedback plays an important role. The commitment that he needs to make is; to give it the required time, be patient, have trust in the HUMAN framework and follow the process. After all, this framework has helped Rohit become a highly-respected leader. He motivates Arun.

Arun feels a little better and asks, "But how will I seek feedback from my team. I cannot go and ask them, you know how my relationship is with them. That is the thing that I need to work on."

Rohit: I understand and that is absolutely fine. The relationship you have with them is not yet good enough to seek feedback directly. You may skip that as of now and only add your own perspective. Once you have a better relationship with your team, you may want to get that feedback and take things to the next level. The framework can work in this fashion as well and please don't feel any pressure about this.

Now, Arun starts feeling ready and motivated to do the exercise. Rohit encourages him to start with the first element, "H". He urges Arun to take his time to complete it. He tells Arun to reach out if he needs any help or clarification.

That evening, Arun takes a print out of the "H" part of the framework and starts filling it out-

Action Time: Heeding Yourself Know Yourself			
Attribute	**My View**	**Feed-back (Consol-idated)**	**Behaviour for Betterment**
Competence	Yes, I am competent. I know the technology and all about project management. Those are the expectations from me.	-	Not Sure
Trust	I think I am trust-worthy. Some team members have ego issues with me and they go to other people when they get stuck on certain points or re-verify the suggestions I have given them with respect to technology. That's their problem, not mine. Ideally, they should consult me and trust my advice, as I am their leader. Sometimes they may feel that I always try to tell them what to do and how to do and that I am controlling.	-	Not to microman-age

Commitment to role	Yes, I am certainly committed.	-	Not Sure
Integrity	Yes, I have integrity.	-	Not Sure
Resilience	Sometimes	-	Not Sure
Do I serve?	Why do I need to serve? I have worked hard for so many years to lead this size of a project, and the team. They should know that I have more knowledge and experience.	-	Not Sure
Caring	Yes, I care about team members.	-	Not Sure
Commitment to team members success?	I suppose I am help-ing team members succeed. Though I want to be the suc-cessful one rather than care about the success of my team members.	-	Not Sure

Admitting mistakes	I hesitate to do so in the presence of my team members.	-	Not Sure
Lead by example	Don't know. My role is different. I cannot lead everything by example.	-	Not Sure
Respect	I am certainly not as popular as Rohit. I don't think my team respects me enough.	-	Not Sure
Say – Do ratio	Yes, I always do what I say.	-	Not Sure

What are the other behaviours that may help me be a better leader?

None that I can think of.

As Arun writes these answers, he calls Rohit and tells him that he is feeling unsettled. He is not sure about the responses that he has written to the questions. He shares with Rohit that he is wondering if these questions will actually help him or make him even more uncertain of himself. He tells Rohit that as a friend, he has a lot of confidence in him and would still like to continue to pursue this framework and he emails the answers to Rohit.

After looking at Arun's "Action Time", Rohit explains to him that it is not just about answering the questions; it is about self-reflection, it is about an opportunity to be introspective and understand oneself better. He explains that a feeling of unsettlement is normal while doing this exercise. He asked Arun whether he gave his hundred percent to the exercise. Arun admits that he wouldn't say he has given his hundred percent. He asks Arun to give it another shot, to be more true to the process, and reflect on behaviours and then write answers. Rohit also reminds Arun to try and put himself in the shoes of his team members when he is trying to answer the questions.

Arun once again gets convinced about the process, and is ready to give it another try.

Action Time: Heeding Yourself			
Know Yourself			
Attribute	**My View**	**Feed-back (Consol-idated)**	**Behaviour for Betterment**
Competence	I am technically knowledgeable in my subject, but I think I am unable to showcase that knowledge in the right way. I get into an argument when I am discussing technical solutions. I object to it strongly, whenever I feel people doubt my capabilities. In the areas where I am not an expert, I try to listen to people, but after a while, I become defensive as I feel the other person thinks he/ she is more superior and knowledgeable than me. I find this difficult to accept. I feel inferior, and behave authoritative to establish my expertise.	-	Listening Skills

Trust	Not sure. I do not think my team members feel that I give them the right advice. Many times, they reach out to others instead of me and quite a few times they recheck things that I have told them. Sometimes they may feel that I always try to tell them what to do and how to do and that I am controlling.	-	Not to micro-manage
Commit-ment to role	Yes, I am committed. I work long hours, and I want to see myself and the company successful. I will do this at all costs. I even tell my team members to work long hours to make this project successful.	-	Not Sure
Integrity	I do have the integrity though perhaps I do not demonstrate that all the time because I shy away from voicing my opinion, particularly to my seniors if the project is going off track. I don't want to face criticism.	-	Not Sure
Resilience	No, I become impatient on many issues and try to deal with the situation by being more authoritative.	-	I need to be more patient

Do I serve?	Sort of. I help the organisation to be successful.	-	Not Sure
Caring	Yes, but I don't want anybody to outperform me. I feel insecure when my team members go to people outside the team and talk about issues, and I know there are people who try to play politics and undermine me. I don't like those team members who talk badly about me, especially outside the team; they are being disloyal to me.	-	Not Sure
Commit-ment to team members success?	Yes, their success is acceptable. But I want to get credit for everything that is happening in the project. If my team goes outside of the channel and take credit for things, which sometimes they do, I feel left out and undervalued.	-	Not Sure
Admitting mistakes	Not in front of anybody in the team; and I am reluctant to show my vulnerability to anyone.	-	Not Sure
Lead by example	Sometimes, for instance, sitting late nights in the office to get the work done, before I ask others to also stay late. However, in general, no, I may not.	-	Not Sure

Respect	I want my team to respect me, but I don't see that happening right now. I feel frustrated.	-	Not Sure
Say – Do ratio	Yes, I always do what I say. When I say we must deliver then we deliver at all costs. I work late in the office, though this is not working well for me in this project because we are behind time and the quality of the work is substandard.	-	Not Sure

What are the other behaviours that may help me be a better leader?

None that I can think of.

Arun sits with Rohit in the coffee break the next day and shares his thoughts with him. Rohit is happy that Arun has taken time to explore and reflect. Rohit conveys to Arun that he has taken the first step. He asks Arun how he is feeling. Arun says that though he is still unsure, he is consciously thinking more about his behaviour and at the same time is feeling overwhelmed as it seems there are many changes that are needed.

Rohit feels empathy for Arun and conveys that he understands fully how Arun is feeling. He conveys this message in multiple ways to Arun, and soon Arun starts feeling comfortable again.

Rohit tells him that it takes courage to observe, reflect and then put these things in writing about oneself. Not everyone can do it, and in doing it, he has shown the desire to change the course of things. He tells Arun to remember that leadership is a journey, and this is the first step of many. He again reinforces that this was exactly how he had achieved full team engagement and he had achieved his success by following the very same path.

He discusses the "Action Time" with Arun to uncover more about some of those behaviours. Also, he motivates Arun for the next step.

Rohit: When you read what you have written; what is that one behaviour that you want to develop right now that will help you to succeed?

After thinking for some time, Arun feels that:

- He has a need to have control over everything that is happening in the project. This may need to be changed.
- And that he wants to stop micromanaging.
- Also, he finds that he becomes impatient with people and does not listen to what they have to say. He feels he needs to improve his listening skills.

Rohit acknowledges and appreciates that he is coming up with behaviours he wants to change. He then asks for details about each of these behaviours like when does this happen, what does he do, how does it have an impact on him and people around him.

After discussing this for almost twenty minutes, Rohit asks him, "What if you have the opportunity to change only one out of these behaviours, which is the behaviour you think would have the greatest positive impact on you and your team at this point of time?"

After giving it a thought, Arun says, "I think working on my listening skills will yield most results." Rohit appreciates that he has come up with the key area he wants to focus on.

Rohit request Arun to fill up the "Action Time" related to Behaviour Change Journey. Arun, takes a few minutes and records his comments in the "Action Time" as below:

Action Time: Heeding Yourself Behaviour Change Journey	
Make a note of the behaviour that you want to change	I would like to work on my listening skills.
How will I demonstrate this behaviour at work? What will be seen and heard?	I will give my team members a chance to speak first. Even if I may not be in agreement with their thought process, I will listen to all they have to say.
With the changed behaviour- How will I feel? How will others feel?	Initially I may have to control myself a lot. I may feel a bit impatient. Others may feel a lot better, since they will get a chance to speak their mind. And it will make them feel important since I will listen to every idea they share as if it is an important idea. I feel that they may feel more satisfied, even if after listening, we discuss and agree to do something completely different.
What opportunities do I have at work to demonstrate this behaviour?	I can exhibit this behaviour at all meetings, interactions etc.
Accountability Partner – Who will help to keep me on track? (Don't hesitate to ask for help/guidance)	Rohit will be my accountability partner. I will discuss my progress with him.
Feedback – Who can provide me with feedback?	Not sure yet.

Rohit explains to him that changing his behaviour is challenging but doable and he introduces him to "Action Time" on "Behaviour Change Journal" where he can log his behavioural changes.

Arun has never written any journal before. Rohit notices his hesitation and again reiterates the benefits and the necessity of doing this. He explains that changing behaviours take time and that the progress is usually slow, that he will need to create an evidence trail for the change as it happens to keep pushing himself forward. All small changes go unnoticed unless given special attention, and that without a journal he may lose hope and leave the process of behaviour transformation.

Arun says that he is keen to change, but he is afraid he may not be able to focus on both changing his behaviour as well as engaging his team.

Rohit smiles and asks Arun, "How committed are you to try this out?"

Arun suddenly feels very comfortable and says, "Well, it is certainly worth a try."

Rohit: If I ask you on a scale of one to ten how important this is to you, with ten being the most important, what would you say?

Arun: It is ten, as I need to survive and thrive in this project.

Rohit: Wow, that's what you need, believe me. Show your commitment and consistently spend some time on it and things will certainly become better. I can tell you that I know for sure as I have been through this myself. All you have to do is to believe in it and continue to follow through to experience the real change. Arun, don't expect miracles to happen if you are not going to change something miraculously. I am sure these are the things which you haven't done earlier but try it once and then let me know if it works or not. I am also putting in effort as I am confident that you can succeed. I know you want to change things and I know I can help you. Ultimately, you are the one who can create the change and make it happen.

Arun: Okay, thanks! I really thank you for helping me. Please guide me as to what I should do next?

Rohit: Practice behaviour change, try to work on your listening skills. Be more aware of yourself when you want to speak. Give opportunity to your team members to speak first. Practice this for a week and make journal entries for first day and a week after that. I hope you can see that there is not much of extra work for you, all your practice is during your routine meetings and discussions, the only thing extra that you have to do is to make journal entries. Also, if possible, try to get some feedback for your second entry that you will make a week later. Let us meet for a review next week.

Arun starts working on his behaviour, initially he forgets many times but starts getting more conscious towards the end of the week. He keeps on reaching out to Rohit and gets some more hints on how to go about this phase.

After practicing listening for a few days, Arun tells Rohit that he becomes a lot impatient, and most of the times he still ends up interrupting his team members. Rohit suggests that during all such discussions, Arun should start taking notes of all important issues that his team members raise, while they are sharing their ideas with him. Rohit believes that this will help Arun's listening skills.

Arun makes the journal entries and the same are reflected below:

Action Time: Heeding Yourself		
Behaviour Change Journal – Listening Skill Improvement		
Parameter	**Day 06**	**Day 13**
Impact on my work How has this change in behaviour impacted my work?	I am trying to become more conscious, so I am able to control when I speak. I haven't found any positive impact on my work so far, rather was uneasy as I was restraining myself from asking what I wanted to ask. I kept quiet and only listened when other people were talking.	Still uneasy about this behaviour change. But practising as per the discussion and commitment to Rohit. Rohit has given a suggestion to help me to listen carefully. As per him, I should take notes whenever something important is being said. I will do that now.
Impact on my team How has this change in behaviour impacted my team?	Didn't find any impact.	Still didn't find any change.

Impact on my work satisfaction		
How has this change in behaviour impacted my work satisfaction?	Nothing	Nothing
Feedback		
What feedback have I received?	No feedback	No feedback
Who provided me feedback?	I couldn't get anybody to provide formal feedback.	I couldn't get anybody to provide formal feedback.

They meet after almost a week and have a quick discussion. Rohit is pleased with the progress and asks Arun, about how he is feeling about it. Arun says that though he is not seeing any results on himself or the team so far, he is committed to continue with the process.

Arun plans to continue working on the framework and requests Rohit to share with him the next element "U" on Understanding with him.

Rohit has to rush for a meeting; he promises to meet him in the evening over coffee.

Understanding Your Team

"Leadership is lifting a person's vision to high sights, the raising of a person's performance to a higher standard, the building of a personality beyond its normal limitations."

-Peter Drucker

U - Understanding Your Team

This part of the HUMAN framework deals with knowing your team members and aligning their roles to the team goals and organisation goals. There are two parts of the element "U" , that will help you achieve this objective:

- The first part is to know the team members individually, as a person, especially their professional and personal aspirations, key motivations, key values etc. This will help you map their expectations from their jobs and career. It will also help you create some synergies and connect with them at a deeper level.

- The second part is about establishing a clear understanding of the roles and responsibilities of your team members and having clarity about the actual contribution of everyone. This leads to higher engagement within the team and enhanced team performance. You should have this understanding and clarity for all team members. You must also make sure that your team members have an equally good understanding of your role and clarity about your contributions, as well as those of the other team members.

Understanding reinforces the principles of fairness and establishes a clear basis for the next stages of the framework. It quells any doubts about favouritism and improves cooperation between team members.

Know Your Team Members

Our own perceptions about how people are may come in the way of establishing the Understanding. It is quite often that we have our own perceptions of people i.e. the way we think about them. When we work with people – our team members or peers, based on our perceptions of who they are, our decisions and relationship with them could be coloured with our perceptions. In other words, we may be affected by our own inherent biases.

As a good leader, it is essential for you to understand people around you and overcome biases if any. It is important to have conversations with them to understand them better. If we make a genuine effort to understand them, we will know how they prefer to work and it will be much easier to help them achieve the best they can.

The idea behind this exercise is to start knowing them as individuals, acknowledge and appreciate their uniqueness, strengths, limitations and diversity they bring to the team.

The leaders who have done this exercise, feel really connected with their teams. Of course, like everything else this exercise has to be done in the right way. Many leaders have given the feedback that they found this exercise far more effective, in making them feel more connected with their teams compared to working on many team building exercises that they have been carrying out for many years.

This exercise presents a really good opportunity for you as a leader to talk to your team members, listen and know more about them. It will help you to have a structured conversation around developing the Understanding about team members.

Once you do this exercise, you will be amazed to see the confidence, empathy and understanding you bring to the table while you work with your team members. The entire process is designed to help bring tangibility to your team's behaviour and expectations. And the beauty of this exercise is that after the first time it becomes so easy to do it, the entire awkwardness just disappears, and it will end up boosting your confidence in yourself. You will also get much deserved respect from your team members when you show genuine interest in knowing them better.

This exercise needs you to talk to your team members in a 1-1 setting. As part of the process you will gather a lot of information. In order to make it more structured, we have identified the areas of discussion, in the "Action Time" below; ideally you can take a print of the form below and use it to fill in the data. You may also add/delete parameters if you feel appropriate. The topics listed below are cues to conversation. There is no specific time limit for discussing a particular topic, and no specific depth that you must go to, you must gauge the interest of the team member for a specific topic and based on that steer the conversation accordingly. It will be great to take notes during these sessions.

The duration of the session could be anywhere from twenty minutes to an hour.

The first discussion may or may not cover all the topics and you may have to schedule another discussion for the purpose of completeness. If you look at the topics below, please do note that this exercise is not designed as a review process and should not become a project or a performance review. It is suggested to ask questions to genuinely explore. There is one specific rule that you must follow, you should not be judgemental, not all people have similar aspirations, goals or family circumstances.

The fundamental thought process behind this exercise is that the discussions will end up revealing some useful data to you, some information that you can use to help team members perform better, work better together as a team and at the same time, keep taking steps to enhance their careers in their chosen direction.

Please use the "Action Time" below:

Action Time: Know Your Team	
Name	
Professional aspirations	
Personal aspirations	
Key motivations	
Key values	

Skill-set	
Communication style	
Professional development needs	
Feedback frequency preference	
Any other information	

Provided below is a brief explanation of all the parameters in the "Action Time" above. It also provides you with cues to start conversation such as some basic questions and some pointers to overcome some known show stoppers.

DESCRIPTION Action Time: Know Your Team	
Parameter	**Description**
Professional aspirations	This parameter gives you an opportunity to understand what aspirations your team member has on professional front. The idea is to gauge what your team members would like to achieve in the next 1 year, 2 years and 5 years. A few questions you can ask to understand this one: • Where would you like to reach in the next one year? • What comes to your mind when you think of yourself after one year? • What are the two career goals for you for the next one year? • After exactly one year from today, what will make you say that this year was perfect from your career stand-point? The list doesn't end here. These are some pointers to start the discussion. Remember it is not an interview, it is an opening of a dialogue. Often the person on the other side may not know what he/she wants in one year. So, asking the same question in different ways will help the other person open his/her mind and come up with what he/she thinks/expects. In case a team member is not clear or has not thought about what he expects on his professional front, you may have to start by giving

examples from your own career, how you achieved the growth that you wanted and what may be your own next steps. This simple act of sharing your story, your struggles and aspirations will allow them to expand their own thinking.

You may even ask them the same question a bit differently as well such as "who do you look up to within the company as a role model?" This could be another way to make them realize, what they really aspire to be.

Also, please do note that in case they are not clear, please do not at any point make them feel less or incompetent. The purpose of this question is to help them realize the importance of setting goals for their own careers and provide them with the comfort that as their leader you are available to help them in this journey.

Do genuinely show that you care and make them feel comfortable.

Personal aspirations	This is to understand what is going on with them at the personal front. What are their dreams? Usually, when a person is asked about his/her personal aspirations, it connects really well with him/her. You could be the first leader who has asked this question and if you listen carefully, you will learn a lot about your team member. It also demonstrates genuine interest and helps you build a better relationship. A few questions you could ask are: • What are your personal goals? • What are you passionate about? • What do you do in your free time? • What makes you happy? Please note the personal aspirations could be about themselves, or their children or parents. Team member may be aspiring to have a big house, a new car, may want to learn singing, or

	want his/her child to achieve a certain career. While you are not responsible for the team member's personal goals in any way, you may find some common elements that you both have interest in. There may be some information or guidance that you can share with them from your own experience, or even facilitate some things without much cost or time. One such example could be that if a team member has aspirations for social work, you can connect him/her with the CSR initiative of the company. Such a move will help the team member gain visibility and career advantage while fulfilling his/her personal aspirations. Any help you extend to the team member will be received with enthusiasm and will help you create a great bond.
Key motivations	Discussion on this topic helps you to understand their motivations. We need to be careful not to underestimate their motivations. Like other aspects of this Understanding part, you need to actively listen and take notes. Be liberal with appreciation wherever you feel appropriate. To start with, here are a couple of questions that you can ask: • What motivates you at work? • What does not motivate you at work? • Who is your role model? • What is that you like about him/her? Do remember to appreciate something that they have done in the recent past, which could be a good start for this discussion. Try to gauge, among the different tasks that your department/ function does, what appeals more to this team member. Everyone has some sweet spot when it comes to work, may be because of unique capabilities, temperament, interest etc.

	This discussion should help you unearth the type of work which this team member would love to do and can excel at, because he/she is inherently motivated to excel at it.
	You may be surprised to discover some hidden talent that you could leverage.
Key values	It helps to have a good discussion of their values. Questions you may use are:
	• What drives you during the day?
	• What gives you energy?
	• What behaviours are most important to you?
	• What bothers you?
	• What values are the most important to you?
	You can use the Value chart in Appendix-1 for an idea on values. You can even show them the chart and ask what values are important to them. The list is not a complete list of values. It is only a suggestive list for reference.
	Values are also an important aspect of a person and it is also very important that the Company Values and Individual Values are aligned.
	A simple example could be Speed of Execution versus Perfection, while some people value delivering as fast as can be, others will value the quality more than quantity. But the important aspect is to understand, what values does the company stand for what is the need of the company from the role that the individual is doing. Many times, individuals are in a role where they struggle everyday due to differences in value systems.
	A discussion with a team member, where you can understand their values could potentially help you create more alignment either by explaining the rationale from the company's perspective and seeking team members' support

	or helping find a right set of responsibilities which are more aligned to individual values.

Furthermore, it may help you understand better any challenging behaviour of a team member. Once you identify why the team member is acting in such a way, you will have the opportunity to help the team member resolve the issue and better align with the company values. |
| **Skill-set** | Discussion with team members will help you to know their own understanding of their skill-set; this should be from both a technical and professional point of view as well as from a soft-skill, leadership and management point of view. All are important.

For example, a person could be delivery focussed. This is his/her strength. Another related strength would be the ability to align each member's delivery to the achievement of a milestone; this would be achieved by engaging with the team and each of the team members.

Remember to be non-judgemental, openly listen and be curious.

Your focus is on understanding your team member; please refrain from providing any feedback at this time.

Following set of questions can get the discussion going:

• What is one accomplishment that you are most proud of and why?

• What strengths did you use in achieving this accomplishment?

• How do you think we could apply these trengths at work?

• How are you feeling when you are saying this? |

	• Any other skills you would like to mention, which you would like to utilise at work?
	You can also enquire about their past successes and probe a little on why they think they succeeded. Many times, you will find that this discussion is not just helpful for you but also for the team member that you are having this discussion with. As explained previously, there is no specific time allocated to any topic, nor is there any limitation on depth of discussion. So this discussion could end up in just as a mutual acknowledgement of the strengths and skills of the team member or could end up becoming a journey to discover the skills. It may even lead to creation of a plan to work on sharpening some skills or a development plan to add some skills that the team member feels are important for him/her to have.
	You may think to assign an additional role if that person is interested to utilise any specific skill they have or willing to develop a new one. You may decide to assign one team member as a mentor for another, based on the capabilities of one and needs of the other.
Communication style	By knowing each person's style, you can customise your approach better, while also helping your team learn how to work more effectively with your own style.
	The communication styles could be assertive, passive, convincing, involving, or inspiring etc.
	You can discuss with the team member about their preferences and also share what you think their communication style is. He/she may discuss openly but often if the relationship is not that developed, people may not feel comfortable to share with you their communication style

	and sometimes they may not even be aware of their style. For some of the relatively junior colleagues it may be a new subject, they may not have the knowledge to understand the different communication styles. If your team members do not share or do not know, you can note down what you think their style is. You can change this parameter in future if you think differently during future discussions. Be sure that once you ask this question, team member will also think about this and may even try to learn more on this. In all cases a discussion on this topic will bear fruits, you will either come out with a mutually agreed better way of communication or a better understanding around what will best work with the team member.
Professional development needs	This helps you to know their point of view on their professional development needs to perform to their best. Some questions to help you start a discussion are as below: • What are the areas that if developed will help you perform better? • What are the things which will help you reach your career goals quicker? You might have noticed by now that many of the topics are linked and like other topics, this topic is aimed at discovering the requirements of a team member in terms of his own development needs, some team members will be able to talk about it, while others will need your help and guidance to determine the best course for their professional development. The options can be training, mentorship, on-job assignment, understudy or even a professional certification supported by the company.

	This particular topic goes together with professional aspirations and any development needs identified must align with the Individual aspirations. For all actions identified, you may start to plan them. A more comprehensive guide on development planning is included in the nurturing part of the HUMAN framework.
Feedback frequency	Having a discussion on this topic will enable you to know what their preferred frequency of receiving feedback is. You may tell them if it is not possible to meet the frequency requested by the team member, but be genuine with your reasons. An early feedback always helps but you have to take this call based on the factors best known to you. Set of questions you may ask to have this discussion going are: • What is the frequency you will prefer for a feedback? • Why do you say so? • How this frequency will help you? Please make sure that once you mutually agree on a review frequency, both of you must make time to enable it.

It is recommended to take notes of the entire discussion, since the discussion may not remain limited to the above suggestions for each topic. This will help you further during the next elements of the HUMAN framework. Also, do not be discouraged in case the discussions do not go as planned and you either need more time to complete the first discussion or you may have to initiate smaller discussions. You may need to put in extra efforts to encourage and build confidence in case the team member does not feel comfortable in discussing or sharing with you.

This is a living document, which means that it should not be treated as fixed. You should look at this document every three to six months and see if something needs to be changed. From second-time onwards, you can merge a few of these topics in your feedback sessions and update the information in this document. In subsequent meetings after the first discussion, it will be quite quick to review any actions that you determine together and update the document with new information or status.

Please ensure that you treat this document as confidential and its contents should not be shared with any third party. You want to build a trusting relationship with your team member and through this exercise you have encouraged them to be open with you. As you want them to be more open, make sure that they know that all discussions are confidential. This will make them feel comfortable to talk to you, to share their success and seek support on tricky or troublesome issues.

As we discussed before, for this exercise to be successful, the team member's active participation is quite important. Since some of you may be doing this exercise for the very first time, team members may have their own doubts and hesitation. In such situations, it is pertinent that you be very careful with the choice of words or sentences, as well as how you conduct this exercise. Listed below are some key points to remember while doing this exercise. Please note this is not an exhaustive list, these are just few pointers and are intended to help you avoid some known pitfalls.

Listed below are some tips for this exercise:

Say Less of...	Say More of...
Last time, it didn't happen...	Wow, it looks good...
You never told me earlier...	I too think that way (only if it is real)...
It is not going anywhere...	How would you call it a success...
You don't have the experience to know how...	Where would you like to be a year from now...
Why would I want to give you this...	We can catalyse each other's thinking...
I know I'll be disappointed...	There's so much to learn from this...

Do Less of	Do More of
Look at the watch	Eye contact
Look uninterested	Responding in between to make sure you are listening
Looking for your kind of answers	Have a genuine curiosity

Day 14: The story continues

As committed in the morning, Arun meets Rohit. Rohit explains the next step that is "U"-Understanding your team, and how important it is to understand the team members. As understanding his team members is not natural for Arun, Rohit explains that this element will make it more objective for him to know his team members. Looking at the element, Arun feels a little uncomfortable and does not want to do it; he explains to Rohit that this looks like a lengthy and time-consuming activity and wonders how it will help him solve his current issues. Rohit reminds him that if he is committed 10/10 for the journey, he has to do these things and once he starts doing them with commitment, he will see the difference.

Rohit advises him to setup meetings with each of his team members to take this forward.

Arun starts planning to organise 1-1 meetings with the team to understand each team member better. Initially, he is hesitant to do so but he gathers courage and decides to give it a shot.

Suddenly he realises that before he does any of this for his team members, it may be appropriate that he does this for himself. He calls up Rohit for a discussion.

Arun: I was wondering if I should try to complete the "Action Time" for myself before I do it for my team?

Rohit: That will be great! It will help you get a lot of clarity on the process and give you a lot of confidence when you talk to your team.

Arun: Is it okay that I reach out to you for a discussion on any issues that I may face?

Rohit: You are most welcome Arun, please feel free to reach out anytime.

Arun thanks Rohit and completes his own "Action Time". He did reach out to Rohit a few times for clarifications and becomes quite comfortable with the "Action Time" by the end of the process.

He then starts first with the most junior members of his team.

He has a discussion with two team members to understand more about them. Arun is surprised that though it is not an easy task to talk about professional and personal matters with a team member, he found that it is very fulfilling once he was through with it.

He finds out through these discussions that his team members have a lot of potential and he did not know this before. He feels that the team is not really comfortable discussing all this but he continues.

Furthermore, one of the team members gives Arun feedback and tells him that he is feeling good after the discussion with him. The team member believed that the questions Arun had asked would be helpful to discover many new things about himself. But the discussion with Arun has made him think about himself and it has been a great conversation. Arun feels on top of the world.

However, he has some tougher conversations with two of his senior most team members, Ashok and Vikas. They are reluctant to speak and share their thoughts. Arun has a hard time remaining patient but remembers his conversation with Rohit and continues the discussion.

With his discussions with Ashok, what surprises Arun is that as the conversation progresses and once Arun shares things about himself, the conversation becomes easier and more pleasant with Ashok. All this is a new experience for Arun.

But the conversation with Vikas seems to be going nowhere. Vikas is not comfortable talking to Arun. He insists he does not have much time and needs to leave in ten minutes. After some heated discussions, the meeting ends. Arun feels frustrated and lost.

He immediately calls Rohit and tells him about his discussion with Vikas. Rohit patiently listens as Arun vents his feelings.

When he finishes, Rohit asks Arun, "What do you think you can do?"

Arun: I really do not have any idea. Can you please help me?

Rohit: What if your manager wants to have this conversation with you, what will be your apprehensions?

Arun reflects and replies, "I will feel uncomfortable suddenly talking about myself because he has not done it before."

Rohit: What is the ideal way you think your manager could start this conversation?

Arun: I would want him to tell me the purpose, his expectations and benefits of this conversation.

Rohit: These are wonderful insights. Did you do that with Vikas?

Arun: I believe I did not do it. No wonder Vikas was very uncomfortable talking to me.

Rohit: Can you please talk to Vikas again by taking him in confidence about what the discussion is going to be about. Vikas needs to feel comfortable and safe. Some level of trust has to be built.

Arun: Okay, but I feel quite uncomfortable sharing with Vikas that I am learning a new framework and as part of that, I may need his help with this exercise. What if he makes fun of me or thinks less of me?

Rohit: It is okay if you let him know that you are trying to improve. When you become a little vulnerable and open yourself to others, they see that as a sign of your trust in them and would usually respond to you in a more trusting way. Please see this as an opportunity to build better trust levels with Vikas.

Arun understands. He decides to meet Vikas again it in a few days.

When he reflects on the day while going back home from work, he feels that for the first time, he has started to build a relationship with his team members, he feels that understanding their drivers and using these drivers to support delivery could help him be successful too. He also acknowledges he is at the early stages of the journey, but so far so good, and he is motivated to continue to work on the HUMAN framework and use this "U" element on all his other team members too.

The next week he requests Vikas for a meeting. This time he explains to him in detail about what he would be doing and how it would help both of them. Vikas agrees to meet and Arun is happy.

Here is some of the data Arun consolidated for some of his team members:

Action Time: Know Your Team				
Name	**Vikas**	**Ashok**	**Vimal**	**Aman**
Professional aspirations	To become Project Director in the next one year	To become Project Director in the next one year	To code something out of the way	To go on-site for longer term
Personal aspirations	To move to USA in the next 3 years	To start my own company in the next 5 years	To do different things	To make more money

Key motivations	Success, Money	To be able to do things independently	Recognition	Money
Key values	Success, Recognition Authority	Independence,- Knowledge, Power Authority	Recognition, Happiness	Work Life Balance
Skill-set	Management Multitasking Technical Skills	Goal-oriented Delivery focused	Quick decision-making and high technical skills	Patience
Communication style	Assertive	Passive	Involving	Passive
Professional development needs	Project management certification Ability to communicate at various levels Listening skills	Project management certification Motivating his team members Collaborating with his team and other stakeholders	Planning	Collaboration

Feedback frequency preference	3 months	monthly	monthly	Monthly
Any other information	-	-	-	He is not at all concerned about his work.

Once you know your team members in detail, i.e., you know about their aspirations, values and motivations, the next step is to do an exercise to outline the roles and create alignment.

Understand the Role and Create Alignment

Generally, this exercise is done in conjunction with HR and may not have been touched for months or even years in some cases. Sometimes, the existing role outline is not valid any more. But as a leader, if you take the exercise forward, it will be another great opportunity for you to connect to your team. The exercise is designed to give a purpose to their role, defining their contributions, limitations, etc.

In a typical project-based technology organisation, these roles could even be only for a particular project or multiple projects if somebody is involved in more than one project.

Doing this part will enable you to give more meaning and sense of purpose to each role. Please have a look at the "Action Time" below that you will use for this exercise.

Action Time: Let's understand the Role	
Name	
Current role/ designation	

Key success indicators (no more than 4)	
Aligned to which key strategic objectives	
Key responsibilities (no more than 4)	
Decision making for this role	

Status update/ reporting expectations	
The next role	

Now, let us understand the above "Action Time" in detail:

DESCRIPTION	
Action Time: Let's understand the Role	
Parameter	**Description**
Name	Name of the team member
Current role/ designation	Role/Designation of the team member
Key success indicators (no more than 4)	Indicate clearly how you will define success for this role.
Aligned to which key strategic objectives	Which of the strategic objectives of department/organisation are these success metrics aligned to. (Defining the bigger purpose)
Key responsibilities (no more than 4)	What are the key responsibilities of this role? What are the primary and secondary responsibilities?

Decision making for this role	What is the decision-making power of this role: • When resolving issues of various types? • For various approvals/go-aheads? Also, mention what are the decisions this role does not have the power to make. • What are the issues for which they should consult you before they take a decision?
Status update / reporting expectations	What are the expectations from the perspective of a status reporting stand point. You may elaborate here the formal status update requirement i.e. if any metrics need to be updated and sent across; if there are any status calls you are expecting your team member to attend etc.
The next role	What is the next role advancement for this role? Mention timelines if possible.

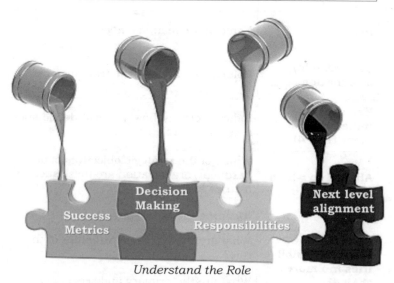

Understand the Role

While doing the above exercise, ensure that the above definitions provide a clarity and purpose to the role. Also, make sure you relate this to the bigger purpose of the team and organisation. All of us connect to our roles much better when there is a strong purpose attached to them.

You should keep these definitions open to be updated at a regular frequency for continuous growth and development.

Here are a few tips for carrying out an effective discussion during this exercise.

Say Less of...	Say More of...
Do not decide yourself...	Let us discuss your perspective...
Don't you even know this...	Let us discuss what you know about this...
That's my job...	What can we do together to 'wow' our customer...

Do Less of	Do More of
Judgement	Giving enough space to talk
Procrastination	Taking the lead
Arrogance	Acceptance

135

Day 28: The story continues

Arun is introduced to the next part about understanding the roles by Rohit. Rohit also shares the related "Action Time" with Arun.

Arun: These are quite detailed and are likely to take up much of my time.

Rohit keeps his cool and says, "when you write code for a project, the specifications are also very detailed. When multiple people work on the same thing, you usually have many documents to record facts so that the end product doesn't lose on functionality and features as per the end client's expectations. Similarly, when multiple people are involved and are working with each other, all of them have one or the other expectation from each other. As a leader, it is important that you make things clear to them. Nothing beats having clarity in black and white."

Arun: I agree, these are very basic things and I think I know these already. Now that you explained this, it has become quite clear. I see more value in doing these exercises. I believe, Rohit, you are an expert and I have a lot to learn from you.

And he is again convinced that this is what needs to be done. As he has some urgent meetings, he decides to do it towards the end of the day. Rohit also advised him to be thoughtful of the bigger purpose of his team, his project, while working on this exercise.

In the evening, he again looks at the document and wonders where to start. He decides to first do this for himself. He starts filling it in and finds that he is not clear about many things.

He starts thinking about the big picture concept, what Rohit had mentioned. He calls up Rohit and checks up with him. Rohit suggests discussing this with his manager and writing it down. But Arun responds that it is not the right time to ask Anupam. He is not yet comfortable asking Anupam as he is experimenting with the framework, and is yet to see any result. Rohit agrees and explores this question with him. Arun reaches a satisfactory answer. Then he completes the whole exercise and he realises that he did enjoy doing this for himself and he expects, so will his team. Technical people value clarity and it brings transparency about everybody's role.

Next morning, the first thing that Arun does is speak to one of his junior team members to discuss the completed form. And the outcome is as follows:

Action Time: Let's understand the Role	
Name	Vimal
Current role/ designation	Technical Lead
Key success indicators (no more than 4)	• Effective and timely delivery • Alignment with stakeholders • Valuable inputs to design • Lower defect percentage (High quality output)
Aligned to which key strategic objectives	• He is helping the client bank to enable their credit officers to sanction loans based on flexible parameters set at a system level. • This helps the organisation to get the project executed efficiently. It is a big ticket project for the organisation. • Adds to a positive reputation for the off-shore team.

Key responsibilities (no more than 4)	• To understand requirements from related documents and Subject Matter Experts, including technical requirements and architecture • To provide module estimates in time • Conduct risk identification • To develop and test a functional and high quality code in a predefined timeline
Decision making for this role	• All decisions related to client, architecture should be discussed with the manager
Status update / Reporting expectations	• Weekly updates to team manager and cross functional stakeholders • To update status on shared drive regularly
The next role	• Recently promoted

From this exercise Vimal realises fully the nature of his role, what he is expected to do and how important it is for the success of the team and the organisation. This has been a helpful conversation and the first time a manager has spent this amount of time and effort for him. He appreciates that in the conversation Arun allowed him to share his thoughts and feels and that they have come to an alignment and agreement. He feels more committed to his job. Vimal shares his appreciation with Arun.

Over the next few days, Arun completes these discussions with all his team members.

He is now very happy about how things are coming together. Arun is starting to see the value of the HUMAN framework.

The exercise's effectiveness also shows up at a weekly project meeting where his team openly discusses status updates and he consciously chooses to listen and not interrupt. He also shares with the team his perspectives and point of view and he feels that it is well received. He feels a better connect. It motivates Arun to take some notes on his behaviour change in his private journal which he has been avoiding doing till now. By end of the day, he willingly opens the journal and commits time to reflect.

Some of the entries from his "Behaviour Change Journal" look like this:

Action Time: Heeding Yourself
Behaviour Change Journal – Listening Skill Improvement

Parameter	Day 06	Day 13	Day 30
Impact on my work How has this change in behaviour impacted my work?	I am trying to become more conscious, so I am able to control when I speak. I haven't found any positive impact on my work so far, rather was uneasy as I was restraining myself from asking what I wanted to ask. I kept quiet and only listened when other people were talking.	Still uneasy about this be-haviour change. But practis-ing as per the discussion and commitment to Rohit. Rohit has given a suggestion to help me to listen carefully. As per him, I should take notes whenever something import-ant is being said. I will do that now	While meeting Vikas today, I found myself to be impatient and not being able to listen. So, I made a conscious effort to listen and take notes, and it helped me to listen to import-ant key points Vikas wanted to share with me about the project. The discussion was actually quite fruitful. Vikas seemed comfortable by the end of the meeting.

Parameter	Day 06	Day 13	Day 30
Impact on my team How has this change in behaviour impacted my team?	Didn't find any impact	Still didn't find any change.	Vikas mentioned today that my being a "patient listener" helped in having an easy conversation and he appreciated that. We shared a good laugh for a change today. I may not have observed other team members. I will notice now.
Impact on my work satisfaction How has this change in behaviour impacted my work satisfaction?	Nothing	Nothing	Because of my discussion and appreciation from Vikas, I felt good about myself.

Feedback

What feedback have I received?	No feedback	No feedback	Vikas said in the conversation "Today you listened to me without unnecessarily arguing for a change." And I take this as a positive feedback.
Who provided me feedback?	I couldn't get anybody to provide formal feedback.	I couldn't get anybody to provide formal feedback.	Vikas

M
Messaging

"The art of communication is the language of leadership"

-James Humes

Messages - Using Right Messages and Stories

Messaging happens all the time; whether this be one-way via a media broadcast or a two-way conversation between two people.

For the purpose of this book, and more specifically the HUMAN framework, a message is a communication from the leader and is intended for his/her people. The type of Messaging can be either verbal through spoken words or non-verbal, the written form. This communication maybe one-way or two-way; primarily determined by the purpose of the message.

Messaging is an important skill to have as a leader and one that can be learnt. We all convey Messages and we do it every day. Some people are able to do this more effectively than others. What is essential in Messaging is:

- Being clear on the purpose of the message
- Planning what one needs to say
- Thinking about the audience and what works for them
- Thinking through how to say it for the best effect.

You must make it simple and straightforward so that when you are delivering the message, your team members get a clear understanding.

Building on from the last element of the HUMAN framework, once you have clear role definitions and you understand your team members (from both a personal and professional standpoint, as well as knowing their aspirations), the next step is for you to design your Messaging or communication to gain better results. It is not that you are going to design the script and deliver that script each day. This is about creating the Messaging for your team that reinforces a connection with you, the team and the organisation. It is also about building trust, motivating and inspiring team members both individually and collectively to go further than they could have ever imagined. It is about engaging your people.

When you talk in a motivating language using the individual and team specific motivations, you enrich the communication and hence strengthen the bond and improve productivity levels.

When you use language that people connect to, messages become much more effective; you create beautiful, effective and everlasting moments.

Developing Messages that Engage and Inspire

Developing messages that engage, mobilise and inspire your team members into action is important. Your messages to them are the critical links that connect them to you, to the rest of the team and to the organisation. It helps them to see a purpose in whatever they are doing at work.

The Messaging element addresses two types of audience:

- Individuals: Messaging at an individual team member level depending on the need.
- Teams: Messaging at a team level to convey the team purpose and targets for the duration/period and inspire and motivate them to deliver.

For the purpose of the HUMAN framework, we have divided the messages in three categories:

- General messages
- Feedback
- Stories

While general messages form the bulk of Messaging that the leader uses, it is equally important to engage with team members and teams using feedback and story-telling. For all of these, we will provide you with a framework to help you craft your message. We will also be providing you some important tips.

Giving the right message is like a muscle, the more you use it, the more you develop and understand it, the easier it will be for you to use it and in time you will be able to flex it as and when you need to.

General Messages

These messages are delivered as part of day to day interactions. Below is a suggestive list of areas for Messaging and this is not an exhaustive list. You can see that these Messaging areas are either at an organisational and/or team level or meant for a team member. We are sure that as you read this list that you will have some areas of your own that you can add:

- Organisation's vision, mission and values
- Organisation's strategic initiatives
- Project goals and milestones
- Co-creating "How we will succeed as a project team?"
- Sharing the project successes, etc.

Below are a few examples of general messages:

- **Vision:** Here is what the organisation's vision is for this year (any other time frame). We all play an important role in the success of the organisation. How would you like to be part of this vision?

- **Key Values:** These are the key values we hold sacred as an organisation (or team or project). How does it fit in with your personal values?

- **Creativity or Innovation:** What do you feel about this project (or product)? How can we make this more interesting?

Our team has shown in the past that together we can bring loads of creativity and co-create things. Let us put our creative hats on, brainstorm together and see how we can achieve this in the required fashion.

- **Goals:** The organisation aspires to reach here (specific goal) within a (specific period). I would appreciate your views on how you think your area (or role or team) can contribute towards this aspiration.

We all need to co-create success together this quarter (or another specific period) and achieve this aspiration of the organisation.

- **Personal commitment or aspirations:** What are your aspirations? What are your aspirations for the project (or team)? How does that align with what we are doing this year?

- **Ownership:** The management team believes that you can do this role. What are your thoughts about it?

- **Journey together, Learning & Celebration:** The organisation has come a long way from where it had started. We shared this journey together and have learned so many things on the way. Let us acknowledge our hard work, success and celebrate this journey. Let us also look at how we can make our organisation more successful in the future.

- **Support:** What can I do to make you successful in your current role? What help do you need from others in the organisation to be successful in this role?

These are only a few examples to help you identify general messages. You may please use them as ideas to design your own messages in the context of your interactions.

Art of Developing General Messages

This part of the HUMAN framework equips a leader to develop the key elements of the message for each team member and each team. This framework considers expectations and motivations of each team member. You can now put to use your knowledge from the work you have done till now to engage each team member in your team to the fullest.

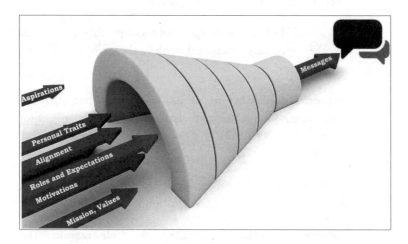

This does not mean that you have to look at a piece of paper and speak to your team members. No, rather you use this as a tool that will aid you to determine what works best for each one of them. It will also give you an opportunity to align your thoughts to their line of thinking.

This exercise of Messaging can also be used for peer relationships to gain better connections.

Individual Messages

A leader needs to craft a set of messages for each of his direct reports. A leader who knows his team members in and out typically also knows what messages he wants to deliver to each one of them. Please remember that as we discovered in the previous exercises, individual communications styles are different, their motivations are different and their aspirations are different too. Therefore, even if the leader has to convey the same message to two of his team members, ideally, he/she should adapt the Messaging to suit the individual concerned so as to make it the most effective.

There are three key elements for each individual message:

- **Individual:** Always use the motivations, strengths, values, and aspirations etc. to tune the message for that person. This will make the person relate to the message.

- **Trust:** Each message must continue to build on the trust between the leader and the team member. The message must convey openness, transparency and concern.

- **Big Picture:** Wherever possible, align the message to things beyond him/her i.e. team, project, vision, strategy, profitability, values etc. This will make sure the individual understands his/her contribution to the big picture and the importance of his/her work.

In the beginning, it may be difficult to tune messages on the fly, it makes more sense to prepare and be ready with the key messages for each of your team members. While we may not always be required to do an extensive planning for communicating messages in each and every case, please make sure that the due diligence is completed for all key messages and key meetings. Like we said before, giving the right message is like a muscle, the more you use it, the more you understand and develop it, the easier it will become for you.

Refer to "Action Time" below for a quick format for "Individual Messaging".

Action Time: Developing Messages	
Name	
Key Messages	

Now, let us understand the above "Action Time" in detail.

DESCRIPTION Action Time: Developing Messages	
Name	Write the Name of the team member
Key Messages	You may write here the list of messages you would like to use for the particular team member at various points in time. You may utilise the suggested message ideas above, based on relevance or may pick up another suitable topic.

Team Messages

As a leader, you need to also deliver team Messages; these Messages are not targeted at any individual in particular and are relatively broad based. So, the prime consideration for these messages is about:

- **Big Picture:** You need to focus on the entire perspective of a situation or an issue. You need to work to align the message to things beyond an individual i.e., a team, project, vision, strategy, profitability, and values etc. This will make sure that the team understands their contribution to the overall goal, the importance of their work and keep them motivated.

- **Co-Creation:** The messages have to be "we" centric, in order to communicate that multiple people/teams are coming together to jointly produce a mutually valued outcome. Using the language of "we" helps reinforce this.

- **Trust:** The message should continue to build trust between the teams/members. Stephen R. Covey, lays a lot of emphasis on trust for great communication, he says "When the trust account is high, communication is easy, instant, and effective." All, leaders must build trust in order to achieve goals. In high-trust relationships, teams communicate well, understand why they are doing things, and are willing to go the extra mile to ensure that goals are met.

The purpose of the team message is that it should impact a large part of the team binding them together. This message should be reiterated at various team meetings to maintain the alignment and connection of the team to each other and the organisation.

Listed below are some tips for this exercise:

Say Less of...	Say More of...
I'll let you know when I need you...	Whom can we ask for help on this...
I'll handle it myself...	How would you handle this...
What could be so hard about that...	We can't get caught up in ego...
I don't want to hear it...	Help me see it from your perspective...

Day 42: The story continues

Rohit explains to Arun the importance of the Messaging part of the framework. He tells Arun that there are many opportunities to engage with his team members using Messaging.

He tells Arun that he needs to reflect on his understanding of team members, prepare and draft the messages accordingly. He must keep in mind the importance of the messages to motivate, engage and connect with the team members at a deeper level.

Arun: How will this Messaging help me in engaging my team?

Rohit: It is a good question. At every interaction, a leader ends up delivering messages to his/her team. Some messages may motivate, some may not. You may have noticed that yourself. Messages may include positive or negative feedback as well. If the messages that you deliver create clarity and are able to connect with people, you will get much better alignment and results. The opposite is true as well. This part of the HUMAN framework enables you to prepare your messages in such a way that you can leverage them to engage your team.

Arun: How do we ensure that the messages connect with people?

Rohit: You will need to align the messages with their motivations, strengths, values, and aspirations etc. to tune the message better.

Arun: Is it primarily based on the information that we acquired during the Understanding phase of the HUMAN framework.

Rohit: Yes, we will use a lot of the information that we collected during previous phases of the framework. In addition, we also use the messages to connect people with the goals of the team, company and align multiple teams together. The big picture, vision, values, mission of the company also play a critical role.

Arun: How will I remember the individual orientation of each message?

Rohit: To begin with, you may maintain notes for individual preferences. You will do this as part of the exercises that follow. Overnight you will not become an expert, but, in time, with practice, you will become really good at it.

Arun: How will I know that the messages are working or not?

Rohit: With time and experience, and the more you get to know your team, you will know when the Messaging is working and when it is not.

Rohit further explains to Arun that Messaging needs to be based on his observations, the importance of the Message to the team member and the team, and has to be delivered at an appropriate time. Most of the general Messaging starts as a conversation, connecting to the team member's values and motivations, sharing how they can add value to the current project success, and seeking their thoughts and opinions to help everyone move ahead.

Doing this exercise seems like an interesting but challenging task for Arun. He is happy with the progress he has made with the HUMAN framework, and the Messaging part seems to take him onto another level though he will have to do his bit to get to this new level of expertise.

He is not confident and is unsure whether he can speak different languages to the team members. He decides that this time he will show enthusiasm and start working based on his understanding. Rohit once again could immediately connect to Arun and understand Arun's hesitation. Rohit demonstrates a use of the Messaging tool immediately by saying, "Look at your courage and determination to use the HUMAN framework, Arun. When many things were not going well for you, you decided to set it all right and you are doing it a methodical and systematic way. This calls for a tribute and a pat on the back. You are using your will and determination to make things happen. That is great, keep the momentum going."

Arun looks at Rohit and he is still thinking.

Rohit: How are you feeling?

Arun: I feel good, thank you. Though I am finding the journey a bit challenging, but your support and guidance helps me to keep going. I really thank you for the motivation.

Rohit: I will be happy when you master this step. Let us meet again in a few days to discuss the next part of Messaging.

Arun finishes his day's work and spends time thinking on preparing on how to implement this part of the framework.

This is when he goes back to the first exercises he had done as part of "H" and "U". He decides to follow the same logic, first to practice by doing this for himself and then applying this to his team. This helps Arun to take the next step.

He tries to imagine himself in a similar situation. Thinking more, he feels that if his manager says things he likes or is driven by, he will definitely be more motivated. He reflects on his conversation with Rohit that afternoon and realises Rohit had used a part of the Messaging element and motivated him today. This is his "aha!" moment and he feels more determined to try it out. He crafts a few messages using what he has learnt from discussions with his team members in the first exercise. He also discusses these messages with Rohit and takes his help for some of them.

Some of the messages he creates are as follows:

Action Time: Developing Messages	
Name	**Key Messages**
Vikas	• The project is at a very crucial stage. Your experience and capabilities in handling projects will definitely help all of us in properly scheduling and achieving timely delivery. • You are good at multi-tasking and management. You can certainly make the project successful with these strengths. What more could you do to manage even better?
Ashok	• Your analytical abilities are very important for all of us. It will be great if you can provide your analytical feedback in team reviews. • Your focus on what needs to be delivered and drive is essential for the success of the team. • How can we use your depth and drive for technology more often in our project? How can it help us to collectively achieve a better quality?
Vimal	• The project is technology driven and complex. Achieving success in this project is a crucial milestone for the organisation. You are going to play a very important role in this. Our SME team appreciates you for being proactive in thinking about different scenarios.

Aman	Message for somebody who is not delivering: • I have been hearing that you are experiencing challenges while working on this part of the assignment, let's talk more about it. • What can I do to help you complete your current assignment? • What are you expecting from other people for this activity? • The reputation with our on-site team is at stake. Delivering this piece of work successfully will certainly help you and us, gain a positive reputation. This will also go a long way in respect to your wish to be considered for an on-site opportunity. You can use this opportunity to showcase that you can work hard and that you have the required capabilities. Please take it more seriously.

He practices this with Vimal. Initially, he feels awkward, but later when the message is delivered; it gives him a good feeling.

He gradually starts doing it with everyone one by one and the team starts responding well to these messages.

Suddenly, one day when he meets Anupam in the corridor, Anupam mentions, "Arun, I have heard that you and your team are working hard and I have also heard good things about you. Keep it up. Let me know if you need any help." This is the moment Arun has been waiting for. He feels good about himself and is now even more committed to the HUMAN framework.

Arun goes through the exercise from "Team Messaging" perspective and designs the messages that he would like to deliver. Some of them are listed below:

• We are co-creating the suite of products which is of the highest importance to our organisation. The success of this project depends on our collective thinking and execution. Together we will make this a success.

- All of us agree that the timelines we have for the project are tight. Also, that it is the real need of the organisation at this point of time. Let's discuss how best we can contribute to this goal. Let's discuss what more resources we need to reach there.

- Imagine how you all will feel when we achieve this goal.

- Our team has a great set of complementary skills, let us collaborate to the full and co-create this success.

- Let us chart out the challenges all of us are facing for our immediate delivery.

- Let us see how we can help each other to overcome challenges. Sometimes when we are in a challenging situation, we don't see ways, while others may. Let us try to solve our team members' challenges in this meeting.

- If time wouldn't have been limited, what could we have done to achieve this goal in the best possible way?

- How can we achieve the above in the given timeline?

Feedback

Feedback is a very specific type of message. Feedback is important at all levels:

- to the individual to know what he/she is doing well and what he/she needs to continue to work on, to be even more effective; and

- to your team to know their performance against the deliverables.

Some leaders avoid giving feedback that are both positive and developmental. Giving feedback is a skill that can be developed. What would be really helpful for a leader is to structurally think through feedback before he/she communicates this to the team member. This element of the HUMAN framework helps you to do that.

Like any other Messaging, it is a must to do your homework and be prepared before you have a conversation with your team member and share the feedback. The frequency of doing this exercise depends on your agreement with your team member. It may be weekly, monthly, or quarterly.

What is important is that you give regular feedback to help your team member to achieve his/her targets. The elements defined in the "U" part of the framework, where you have identified the traits of your team members may help you. For example, if by doing the "U" part for a member, you realise that a particular team member will work best if given feedback frequently, then you must follow that frequency.

Getting Ready for Feedback Session

You need to plan your feedback session. The important question to ask yourself is, what outcome do I want at the end of the conversation? It should ideally be that you have had an effective conversation and have agreed to a way forward to help strengthen the team member's performance and help him/her meet or exceed his/her targets.

A very important aspect of feedback is that it is not personal, it is work related. It must be objective and related to work. Feedback is not a measure of someone's capabilities; it is based on the role and expectations against deliverables. Frequently, people confuse it with capabilities. It is your responsibility as a leader to clarify that the particular person is in their role because he/she is capable. The feedback is on what, how and when the work is delivered as well as the way forward.

4W model explained below can help you structure the feedback and is as follows:

1. **Where are we going?**

   This part starts the dialogue and breaks the ice by getting everyone on the same page about where the team or organisation is headed to. Provide not more than five sentences to explain this part. You can talk about business targets, customers, test results, implementation targets or any other parameters as applicable. As a leader, you should also be prepared to answer queries on this one.

2. **Where is the team member going?**

   Then talk about the individual you are addressing. What is his/her progress against the work expectations? The initial part should be to ask the person what does he/she thinks about where he/she is going. Then you need to share your feedback about what you think as a leader and provide your assessment of the situation. This discussion allows both you and your team member to align and have the same understanding of what is expected.

3. **What is going well?**

What are the things the team member is doing well? Make sure to highlight the points where that individual has performed as expected and the areas where he/she has exceeded the expectations.

4. **Where can we improve?**

What are the gaps, and how can both the parties work together to fill the gaps? The best way to put this is to ask:

- What is not going so well?
- Where are the gaps?
- How do you think we can fill the gaps?
- What are the things you can do differently?
- How can I help?
- Shall I make some suggestions? And then you can use the opportunity to share your suggestions as well.

To prepare for the feedback conversation based on the 4W model, please use the following "Action Time". The parameters in the "Action Time" will help you jot down pointers for all the four parts of the 4W model. This is not to be shared with the team member. The data in the below "Action Time" will make you ready with the essential elements of the feedback that you want to communicate. Many times, the feedback discussions do get derailed and some of the important points are missed out. Once you are ready with a structured content, the likelihood of missing important elements of feedback reduces and the feedback session becomes more productive.

The below "Action Time" is not meant to define the structure of the conversation. For creating an effective structure, please use the 4W model above. This "Action Time" will just help you to collect your thoughts in regard to the model above.

Action Time: Feedback	
Name	
Expected feedback session time frame	
Team goals and expectations	
Role expectations	

What is going well?	
Supporting behaviour and cases	
Area of expectations mismatch	
Supporting behaviour and cases	

What do you want them to do differently?	
Any timelines?	
What happens if he/she does things as you suggest?	
What happens if he/she doesn't?	
What support does he/she need from you?	

A brief explanation of the different elements of the "Action Time" above is as follows:

DESCRIPTION	
Action Time: Feedback	
Parameter	**Description**
Name	Name of the team member.
Expected feedback session time frame	When is the feedback session planned?
Team goals and expectations	What are the overall objectives?
Role expectations	Note down the expectations from the role.
What is going well?	Note down what the team member is doing well during the review period.
Supporting behaviour and cases	Add details of examples supporting above statements.
Area of expectations mismatch	Note down areas, where the team member does not meet your expectations
Supporting behaviour and cases	Add details of examples supporting the above statements.
What do you want them to do differently?	What do you think is their issue and how do they go about fixing it, what things should the team member do differently?

Any timelines?	Provide timelines/define milestones for progress on the above.
What happens if he/she does things as you suggest?	Provide benefits of compliance, this may be an incentive or benefit that the team member will receive.
What happens if he/she doesn't?	Provide consequences for non-compliance, let the team member know what they will be losing on, in case they do not meet expectations.
What support does he/she need from you?	Please note what help the team member might need from you or what help you can extend to the team member.

Please do note that the above "Action Time" is not to be shared with the team member, the only purpose for it is for you to prepare for the feedback session.

There will be some actions coming out of the discussions, please take a note of them and ensure that the relevant actions are completed before the next feedback discussion.

All organisations also have their formal performance review discussions; these are the formal occasions to provide feedback. The organisations may also provide guidelines, parameters and processes to support such review sessions. Please continue with such sessions as required. The feedback part of the HUMAN framework provides for more informal discussions and a continuous channel for engaging team members and helping them in making progress. You may adopt some of the elements of feedback provided here into your organisations performance review constructs. You will note that it will help you connect better with your team members.

In the tables below are listed a few do's and don'ts for the Messaging around feedback.

Say Less of...	Say more of...
You didn't do this...	Co-create...
See, I told you...	How can we do it...
This just does not happen here...	I am sure you want to do it...
I knew you would falter...	I won't be angry if you put the real issues on the table — we're in this together...
There's no way this will fly here...	If we "pilot" it and it doesn't work, we don't have to adopt it...
You can't...	Let's talk about how to make it happen...
Stop questioning me...	You've got permission to challenge me...

Do Less of	Do more of
One-sided talking	Listening
Talking about yourself	Talking about the team or team member
Interrupting	Being with them
Mechanical feedback	Involved feedback – human to human

Day 56: The story continues

Now it has been almost two months since Arun has been implementing this framework. Arun focuses on the feedback part of the framework. He knows that he generally becomes defensive while taking and giving feedback. He discusses this with Rohit and Rohit explains that he was also like that when he started working on this framework. However, using the framework has not only improved his feedback giving skills but also feedback-taking skills. Now he is much more proactive in taking and giving feedback in a manner which is relevant to the team. Arun could never imagine that Rohit could ever be like that, but he still tries to believe what Rohit just said about himself. And he feels motivated by thinking that if Rohit has transformed, he also has the chance to do so. Rohit explains that it will take time and practice.

Arun: Interesting, but feedback is a difficult thing, isn't it?

Rohit: You may feel uncomfortable in the beginning. With time, you will become more aware of your feelings and team member's feelings and gradually you will master the skill.

Arun: I have noticed that feedback generally discourages people; even my own discussion with Anupam was a bit scary.

Rohit: Feedback is actually a very positive tool. But like any other tool one needs to learn the right way of using feedback. This is the time when you can co-create a way forward for mutual success. Like other elements of the HUMAN framework you will get an "Action Time" to support you.

Arun: Usually people do not easily connect with feedback.

Rohit: I agree, but in the HUMAN framework, we have been progressing step by step, you have already spent time knowing yourself and understanding your team members. Now you have the context. Had you provided feedback abruptly, it may not have provided positive results.

Rohit further guides him to do this exercise for this project. He informs Arun that the "Action Time" here is only for your analysis and preparation for the feedback meeting. This "Action Time" should not be shared with your team members and other stakeholders. He advises Arun to prepare feedback for his team and have supporting observations for the feedback before he schedules the conversation.

Arun works on the "Action Time" and comes up with the following data for his feedback discussion with two of the team members, Vikas and Ashok.

Action Time: Feedback	
Name	Vikas
Expected feedback session time frame	Monthly
Role expectations	• Responsible for the design of the module as the technology lead. • Develop good relationships with other stakeholders like SMEs, testing teams and on-site teams. • Inform and discuss with stakeholders when there are issues.

What is going well?	He is doing well on his module. So far, his design has been accepted well and there have been no complaints. He is able to take care of the end to end integration of the module with the whole product.
Supporting behaviours/cases	• Don't have any complaints from the on-site team. • Progress of his part of the project is on track.
Area of expectations mismatch	He bypasses me when it comes to issues, he wants to showcase that he is more in sync with technology than me.
Supporting behaviours/cases	When there was a difference of opinion last month between the technology team and the SME's (Subject Matter Expert) , he discussed and clarified the technology issues without sharing details with me.
What do you want them to do differently?	To discuss and highlight issues to me.
Any timelines?	I expect that he gets more comfortable within one month and starts discussing with me on the issues/challenges he faces in the project.
What happens if he/she does things as you suggest?	I will feel happier and informed. I will make sure that he gets all the support that he needs to make the project successful. There will be more trust on each other. We all will be equally informed when talking to other stakeholders on the project. We can utilise our learnings to other parts of the project.

What happens if he/she doesn't?	People outside project will think that I don't know anything and I don't have control over my team. I will stop trusting him and try to divert work away from him.
What support does he/she need from you?	I need to build rapport and, trust with him.

Action Time: Feedback	
Name	Ashok
Expected feedback session time frame	Quarterly
Role expectations	• Take responsibility of the design of his module as a technology lead. • Develop relationships with other stakeholders like SMEs, testing teams and on-site teams. • Inform and discuss with me when there are issues.
What is going well?	He is good at technology. His drive to learn more and more about technology is quite impressive.
Supporting behaviours/ cases	He reads a lot on technology and is always updated on the latest technology. The on-site team is quite happy with his in-depth knowledge and his ability to stitch various modules together.

Area of expectations mismatch	He competes with his team on technology, which demotivates people.
Supporting behaviours/ cases	• It is noticed at the meetings that he lets his team down and argues if somebody else uses technical knowledge to counter him. • He uses his position and authority for ignoring their suggestions, opinions and overriding their inputs.
What do you want them to do differently?	To discuss issues with me.
Any timelines?	I expect that he gets more comfortable within one month and starts discussing with me the issues and challenges he faces in the project.
What happens if he/she does things as you suggest?	I will feel happier and informed. There will be more trust on each other. We all will be equally informed when talking to other stakeholders on the project. We can utilise our learning to other parts of the project.
What happens if he/she doesn't?	People think I am unable able to lead these intelligent people properly. I might have to take a bigger role in some more of the projects to make sure that he keeps me in the loop. I may have to micromanage some of the aspects.
What support does he/she need from you?	I need to build rapport and trust with him.

Arun used this data to have his feedback discussions with these two team members. He was surprised to see that he could understand their concerns and was able to address them without getting into arguments. He did not have to use his authority to try and make them compliant, something that he had tried to use unsuccessfully in the past. In fact, by preparing for the meetings, he had created a clear picture in his mind as to what he really wants to achieve in the discussions. His openness and clarity of thought about what he wanted and why, was enough to convince his two team members to align themselves with his thought process in the interest of the project and the success of their team. Arun promises himself to continue to put in efforts and regularly practice all aspects of HUMAN framework that he has learned so far.

Share Stories that Engage and Inspire

Storytelling is a powerful leadership skill that helps inspire, engage and motivate team members towards reaching their own goals and the overall team goals. In the daily rush of activities, many leaders underutilise storytelling. This mode of Messaging sets a vision, teaches important lessons, defines culture and values, and explains who you are and what you believe in.

This part of the HUMAN framework provides you the tools that enable you as a leader to spend some time beforehand and note down the stories which you may want to share with your team to inspire them towards their goals and be more effective.

Some key aspects to think about:

- When will a story be the best way to communicate?

- Who should you be telling it to?

- What do you want to achieve as a result of telling the story?

- Where and how best to tell the story?

The most important aspect of storytelling is being able to tell the story genuinely, bringing in something of yourself when you share the story.

How to Share an Inspiring Story?

Sharing an inspiring story is an art and a science. To get the best results one must focus on the following three main elements:

- Context
- Action
- Result

A brief explanation of these elements is provided below:

Context

The context provides the background information, the circumstances, the setting of an event etc. so that listeners understand the relevance of the story. It should trigger their interest and make a connection so that they care about what you have to say.

Context should address four questions:

- When and where does the story take place? Is it a fact or fiction?
- Who is the main character? Is this the person, the listener needs to connect with? In most cases this maybe you.
- What does he/she want? Explain what he/she wants to achieve.
- What is the challenge?

Action

Every inspiring story has action (just like in an action movie) in which the main character braves conflicts, failures and setbacks. The true action is when we feel and experience the character's story and learn lessons from the story.

Result

At the end of the story, you must reveal the outcome for the character. You should explain, though subtly, what your listeners should have learnt. What is the moral of the story? Why did you tell the story?

Some Tips

Great storytellers know that a powerful story is only one part of what inspires people to listen. Follow the tips below to become a better storyteller:

- **Observe:** Actively watch and listen to great storytellers and see how they construct, connect with their listeners, and share their stories. These experiences will help you to be a great storyteller.

- **Listen:** The best storytellers are the best listeners. Develop your listening skills and give others your full attention when they tell a story.

- **Practice:** Rehearse your story before you tell it. Even if you practise on your own, just once, in front of a mirror or video camera, this can improve your storytelling skill greatly.

- **Create an experience:** When you tell a story, you create an experience for your listeners. Appeal to all the five senses by using words that create imagery for each one of the senses, don't just tell them.

Tell Stories that engage and Inspire people

Stories You Plan to Share

You must decide what stories you want to tell and collect the relevant stories, some of the suggested topics are listed below:

- Overcoming a challenge
- Learning from success
- Learning from challenges
- How a team banded together during tough times
- Journey of the organisation or team
- The best leader in your work history, and what you learned from that experience
- The worst leader in your work history, and what you learned from that experience

The following "Action Time" will help you create a list of stories:

Action Time: Stories to Share	
Name	**Stories to Share**

Name	Stories to Share

The following table provides a brief description of the parameters:

DESCRIPTION	
Action Time: Stories to Share	
Name	**Stories to Share**
Write the name of the individual or team	Write briefly the relevant context and an indicator to the story you want to share. Also, briefly indicate what is the inspiration you want to drive.

You may plan to update your list every six months or so. You may come across interesting experiences that may have relevance to your context. Feel free to adopt from the experiences that others share with you.

Day 84: The story continues

As Arun has been into the process for almost three months, he is feeling more comfortable with the team. When he talks to his team members, he is more aware of himself and them. Sometimes it creates additional pressure on him as he is more aware and has to manage a few aspects of his behaviour, but he is very happy with the change in his team's behaviour. The Messaging part of the HUMAN framework is helping him in a structured way to engage even better with his team and to support the delivery of the project.

In the next meeting, Rohit briefly introduces Arun to the storytelling and requests him to look at the "Action Time" and plan some stories to share with his team.

Arun also remembered that Rohit keeps sharing stories about himself as well as others. One of the stories he remembers was the one that Rohit shared when he mentioned that he was very defensive himself and how the HUMAN framework has helped him overcome this limitation. And when Arun had heard this, he had felt motivated to do the feedback exercise. Arun comes up with his own list of stories for some team members to help motivate them in the same fashion that he has been motivated by Rohit. Below listed is a partial list of stories he came up with.

Action Time: Stories to Share	
Aman	I have observed that Aman is less engaged. I can tell the story about how a member of another project has been selected by the on-site team because the performance of the selected person far exceeds in the expectations for the project.
Ashok	To motivate Ashok to adopt the HUMAN framework, so that he can deal with his people more effectively. The story about myself and how I changed in the last few months by getting help from Rohit who was an expert at it.
Vikas	When Vikas is demotivated, and frustrated by discussions with the testing team, I should be able to motivate him by explaining how in my last company, one of the successful teams had the best results as their project lead had the skill of managing all stakeholders. By thinking from stakeholders' perspective and aligning their goals and our goals, ultimately they become the shared goals.

In the meantime, Arun notices that the team has built a greater rapport with him. He has become more observant of his own behaviour. He is also constantly monitoring his behaviour of listening.

Arun's on-site partners are very pleased and satisfied with the progress.

Acknowledging

"People often say that motivation doesn't last. Well, neither does bathing – that's why we recommend it daily."

-Zig Ziglar

Acknowledging

Acknowledgement is a powerful tool to be used in business. A leader uses this tool to engage team members in an effective manner. It also creates a positive culture and reinforces a sense of belongingness. Furthermore, it motivates people to keep striving to deliver the best business results. It is a tool that all leaders are aware of, but either tend to underutilise or tend not to recognise the importance of and sometimes both. It is a universal truth that people appreciate and respond positively to Acknowledgement.

Abraham Maslow published a theory in 1943, that humans have five basic needs. His research named, "A Theory of Human Motivation" was published in the journal Psychological Review. Esteem is one of them. In Maslow's own words, "All people in our society (with a few pathological exceptions) have a need or desire for a stable, firmly based, (usually) high evaluation of themselves, for self-respect, or self-esteem, and for the esteem of others. By firmly based self-esteem, we mean that which is soundly based upon real capacity, achievement and respect from others. Satisfaction of the self-esteem need leads to feelings of self-confidence, worth, strength, capability and adequacy of being useful and necessary in the world."

In short, esteem leads to the feelings of self-value and self-worth. Acknowledgement is a great tool for leaders to help make the team members feel valued and worthy.

We would like to classify Acknowledgement into two parts:

- Formal organisational level initiatives
- Leader led initiatives

Formal Organisational Level Initiatives

There are formal organisational initiatives to acknowledge employees and teams. As part of these organisational initiatives, leaders may make nominations/recommendations for the relevant Rewards and Recognition (also known as R&R) programs. Also important is the part that is related to annual increments, bonuses, cash rewards and incentives. While some of the formal processes are mandatory and every leader should participate in them, quite a few are optional and a leader can use these formal processes at his/her discretion.

It is necessary that leaders are constantly in touch with HR or concerned teams to stay updated with respect to these organisational processes. They should take interest and use these initiatives as applicable.

Leader Led Initiatives

In addition to the organisational tools available to you as a leader, there are many other ways in which you could recognise your team members. How well you use these additional ways, is totally dependent on your own interest and initiative. As a good leader, you should have your own strategy on Acknowledgement.

Crafting an Acknowledgement Strategy

This element "A" (Acknowledging) of the HUMAN framework helps you to design an Acknowledgement framework for your team members that will motivate them to drive the business to success for themselves, their teams and the organisation.

As a first thing, you as a leader should be thoroughly aware of your organisation's rewards and recognition system. Please make a note of all the kinds of formal reward programs that are available to your teams and when can you utilise them.

Generally, these rewards systems are designed at the organisational level. Depending on your role and flexibility of the organisation, you could use this element to align rewards to individual team members.

As discovered in the previous parts of the HUMAN framework, each individual's aspirations, motivation and values differ, so it should not come to you as a surprise that they have their own preference for the way they get acknowledged. Their response to Acknowledgement may also differ.

Understanding what motivates each team member when it comes to Acknowledgement is even more relevant when there are multiple generations at work. It holds true that what works for a team member who is close to retirement may not work for a young, new graduate.

Acknowledging in a way that a person wants to be acknowledged not only motivates, it also makes the person feel that he/she is working towards a bigger objective. It gives a feeling of self-worth, belongingness and fulfilment.

If your own manager does acknowledge you in the right way, you can take some cues from it and learn from your own experience and if he does not do it well, look into your own heart and you will find a longing there, take a cue from it and you will know what your team members may be missing. You may learn from your own experience and make a commitment to acknowledge more often.

While we are on this topic, please note that there is always a possibility that you may start evaluating your own situation as individual versus those of your team members for all the other elements of the HUMAN framework also. You may find that you can actually use some of the good things that your manager does and implement them as part of your own HUMAN framework that you develop for your team.

This part of the framework is designed to help a leader develop an Acknowledgement strategy for his team. The following format may be used to capture the required information for each of the team members.

Action Time: Acknowledgement	
Name	
What?	

Why? (Supporting facts to share)	
How? (Acknowledgement method)	
Who? (Stakeholders need to be involved)	
When?	

Provided below, are details of this "Action Time", this will help you understand the importance of each of the elements of this "Action Time". Subsequently we will see this "Action Time" as part of Arun's story and it will help you get further clarity about how to use this "Action Time".

DESCRIPTION Action Time: Acknowledgement	
Parameter	**Description**
Name	Name of the team member.
What?	What is to be acknowledged or appreciated?
Why? **(Supporting facts to share)**	The most important thing when you acknowledge and appreciate people is to make it more specific about the incidence, success, way of being etc. This makes your appreciation more authentic and appropriate. It strongly reinforces the good behaviour and work. Please do note that these incidences/facts do not have to be a big one. Small things, small behaviours, small acts, gestures etc. can also be mentioned.
How? **(Acknowledgement method)**	It is to mark a couple of their preferred way of Acknowledgement. There are a few ways you can do it- you can sense it while working with them and fill this here and try it out. Or you can tell them that you are collating this information as part of your leadership exercise and ask them. E.g. By email or in a meeting or in an open-house etc.

Who? (Stakeholders need to be involved)	Who are the people who should know about this acknowledgement or appreciation?
When?	You can put a time frame for when you want to acknowledge or appreciate.

A few points to consider for this specific element of the HUMAN framework are listed below:

- A good leader always finds small reasons to acknowledge his/her people.

- At no point, your team member should feel that he/she is getting the Acknowledgement because you are a great leader or because of your magnanimous nature, or that you are doing them a favour. The highlight of the Acknowledgement is the team member not "You".

- Please make sure that Acknowledgement conveys that the team member is receiving it because he/she truly deserves it, please do not shower undue praise.

- The team member is only getting what they really deserve and they should not be made to feel obligated in any way.

- Don't at all play favouritism. Let your Acknowledgement be fair.

- Acknowledgment cannot be equated with the casual words of encouragement; those casual words may not be enough.

Fear of Acknowledging

Some leaders may not be comfortable in frequently acknowledging good work. There may also be a fear that in case you always acknowledge good work, team members may lower their standards and not deliver up to the mark in future.

In our experience, sometimes you may not be sure of what to do and what to expect, because it may not have happened before and there may be a fear of getting into an unknown territory.

But we strongly encourage you to find reasons to acknowledge each of your team members. If you do it for just six months, it will become a habit for you and your mind will start automatically working this way.

Given below are some tips for you to avoid some common mistakes and have great conversations as part of this exercise.

Say Less of...	Say More of...
You are one of the many award winners...	You have helped the team...
Anybody could have done this...	Your behaviour has made a difference...
I appreciate you ...	You are being appreciated...
I recommended you for this one...	You deserve this reward...

Do Less of	Do More of
Getting self-limelight	Appreciating with specifics
Envy	Highlighting team members' success
Being miserly with appreciation	Frequently appreciating

Day 116: The story continues

Arun is now four months into the framework. Arun and Rohit meet after work for a quick catch up.

Rohit: How are you, Arun?

Arun: It feels that I have come a long way already!

Rohit: What more can you tell me?

Arun: A lot actually, I am happy to share that I did get some appreciation from Anupam. He mentioned that he has been getting positive signals from the on-site team. Also, the team has indicated that they like the "new me". They now have reasons to believe that I am genuinely interested in their own betterment. I have been getting positive signals about all the new initiatives that I have taken up.

Rohit: How did you feel getting acknowledged?

Arun: Thinking about it, it is one of the best things that could have happened to me. All the hard work and special attention that I have been giving to learning more about myself, about the team and the efforts I spent to deliver the right messages to align the team, suddenly feel very valuable.

Further discussing with Rohit, Arun understands that acknowledgement, appreciation and recognition are important. After all, he felt pleased when Anupam told him that he had noticed a change in his behaviour over the past two months; and that the team was starting to deliver quality work, on time. And that he had heard from people that Arun was more engaged with his team members.

Rohit: Why is it important to acknowledge your team and team members?

Arun: I believe it is very simple, everybody feels happy if they are acknowledged and appreciated.

Rohit : What else?

Arun: They also feel more motivated towards work.

Rohit: Yes, you are right. Based on my experience, it also makes them feel important. And also tells them that the leader is unbiased, and notices not just everything that goes wrong, but also what is done well.

Arun: Wow, I never thought about it in such depth.

Rohit: You must also understand the organisational initiatives for rewards and acknowledgement. I suggest you meet the HR team and then we can connect again in a few days.

Arun knows that there are formal organisational ways to acknowledge his team members. So, he agrees with Rohit that before he thinks more about his own way of structuring individual Acknowledgement within his team, he must talk to the HR about what is in place and available to him as a leader.

After the meeting with HR, he then sits down to see what structure he could put in place to acknowledge his team members and his overall team. He also reflects more deeply on his own leadership journey and the conversations with Rohit, using the framework HUMAN.

He starts to reflect on an Acknowledgement structure that he could use. He tries to understand the Acknowledgement "Action Time"; and as usual, after a week, sits with Rohit to have a discussion.

Rohit: You told me that you had a discussion with HR on rewards. What happened?

Arun: Yes, I had a discussion and figured out that there are three awards which can be applied for my team members and one award for the team. It will happen at quarter end and they will send an email on it. I will take care of it when time comes.

Rohit: That's great. How about Acknowledgment "Action Time"? What did you think of that?

Arun: By the way, I don't think it is overwhelming.

Both of them share a laugh.

Arun: I have been looking at it since yesterday and found it quite interesting. I haven't yet started work on it. Can we go through the "Action Time" together?

Rohit: Sure, you definitely understand the importance of it. I am sure you will do a good job on it. How would you find out their preferred way of Acknowledgement?

Arun: Do you want to share your experience working on this one?

Rohit: Some of my team members prefer a public Acknowledgement, such as a special mention at a team meeting, in the presence of their peers and their own teams, they feel that such acknowledgements are very authentic. While some others value an email where I copy some of my own peers involved in the project, they feel that this will give them an opportunity to be known beyond our team and help them build new relations as well. There could potentially be other preferences as well.

Arun: Sounds good. I will start working on this.

Rohit: Apart from specific Acknowledgment for team or team members, you could regularly also thank them in general for the efforts that they put in.

And their discussion continued.

After the discussion, Arun decides that he will implement the following as part of his plan to acknowledge the team in general:

- At the end of every week before leaving office, he will say thanks to his team members for the week and wish them a lovely weekend.

- At team meetings, while going through the action list, he will say thank you when an action is completed.

He also creates an Acknowledgement strategy for his team members, one such "Action Time" is reproduced below for your reference.

Action Time: Acknowledgement	
Name	Vikas
What?	Has been doing great work on technical architecture.
Why? **(Supporting facts to share)**	He has successfully completed an important milestone by completing the design and architecture document. The document has been appreciated by the on-site team for its thoroughness and quality.
How? **(Acknowledgement method)**	Appreciate in front of people as well as sending an email to the group, acknowledging him as a the star of the fortnight for reaching this milestone.
Who? **(Stakeholders need to be involved)**	My team members, peers supporting this project and the on-site stakeholders.
When?	Email to be sent before the quarterly project review with all stakeholders. And verbal acknowledgement during the quarterly project review.

A month later Arun meets Rohit. Arun is excited about his progress and wants to share it with Rohit. He tells Rohit what has been happening and more specifically what he has noticed within the team and the overall impact of the systematic approach of the HUMAN framework. He is pleased with the progress and has a wonderful feeling of achievement.

Rohit smiles and congratulates Arun, that so far, Arun has successfully been able to transform a disengaged team to a team that is engaged and performing. Rohit also explains that Arun has one more step in his journey with the HUMAN framework, that of "N" (Nurturing). That Nurturing is an equally important step, building on the other elements. It focuses on people development.

Rohit reminds Arun that at their level in the organisation leading and managing is the largest component of their role. Building leadership competencies on top of technical competencies may be hard; however the success that Arun has achieved in a short time is a testimony to the transformational power of the HUMAN framework. Furthermore, Rohit mentions that he himself has never stopped revisiting the framework as it has been a great tool for his own success as a leader.

Nurturing

"*Before you are a leader, success is all about growing yourself. When you become a leader, success is all about growing others.*"

-**Jack Welch**

Nurture Team Members

In continuation of your efforts to engage your team, the next step for you is to connect their day to day work with their own long-term goals and aspirations.

Nurturing is the last part of the HUMAN framework and is quite significant in the support that it lends to all the previous elements of the framework. The simplest analogy is that of the person, who owns a fruit plantation, the initial process of the planting, watering, regular caring for the saplings is rewarded over time, many times over, and the trees once developed do provide much more than fruits, they remain useful even after they have completed their meaningful life. Also, do remember the shade that they offer to a passer-by, the shelter they provide to birds, the general contribution they make to the environment and well-being and peace they convey to everyone who sets their eyes upon them. Well rooted trees can also prevent floods and save the soil strata.

In other words, if you really want to enjoy the fruits (results that your team can achieve together), you must work hard to care for them, nurture them.

You may argue that this analogy is a bit incomplete, since the needs of the trees are very simple and known and you know for sure that the fruits will be yours at the end of the toil, but the same may not be true for people.

When it comes to people, many times it is very difficult to ascertain what the best is for an individual and you also have to take care of the organisational dimension. Sometimes, the needs of the individual may not align with the needs of the organisation and may cause a conflict.

Then there is also the fact that your team members may move on to new roles and in future, may not work for you anymore, so is it worth spending time and energy on developing them?

Also, as your role evolves, you need team members who can assume greater responsibilities. You may either help them develop and grow with you and or just get new people with the right experience and skills to manage the role. Which one is better? Is hiring better or developing?

In summary, is it worth taking all this trouble?

Technology people will always be looking at such dilemmas as they try and compare various alternatives and may choose the lowest cost or the fastest method.

Well, let us take an example from the story of Abraham Lincoln regarded as one of the most important presidents in American history. He was well known for his energy and productivity. Lincoln's insistence for using sharper tools to get the job done always resulted in more efficiency. He said, "Give me six hours to chop down a tree and I will spend the first four sharpening the axe."

Lincoln, who was actually a skilled woodcutter before becoming president, probably meant this literally as well as figuratively. Inefficient tools end up wasting energy. It is always better to spend the majority of your time finding and cultivating the best tools for any task.

Remember that in today's world the leader's strength lies in his team! The more you work on your team, the more engaged they become and easier becomes your job.

Moreover, the more you can help your team members grow and develop, the more you will be able to strengthen your team, delegate more tasks and move on to more ambitious challenges yourself.

Please remember that engaged team members, especially the ones that are nurtured and cared for like those trees we mentioned above, not only deliver best results but also:

- Offer support to others
- Charge the environment by their infectious enthusiasm
- Help groom other team members
- Are a pleasure to work with and all customers that interact with them are happy
- They are also the ones who solidly believe and connect with the company and provide stability during turmoil (internal or external)
- And even when they leave you, they spread good words about you as a leader and would motivate others to work for you, recommend best people to you and continue to lend support to you

If you remember the time that you spent helping some team member grow, you will instantly realise that this investment has yielded the most results and that none of your effort has been wasted, in fact you may be proud of the progress that the team member has made. You may quickly realise that those moments when your team members succeeded, make you proud even today.

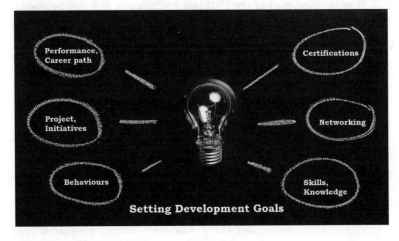

Setting Development Goals

Development Planning

Development planning offers a simple, powerful way to help both you and your team members think about the future. A development plan explains how a team member will grow professionally, and lays out a plan for him or her to follow.

Every organisation has formal individual development plans, and most of the time, organisations also define the processes, formats and timelines for development planning. But in our experience, a lot of times, leaders do not use them effectively.

However, as part of the HUMAN framework, the development planning is a key activity and is strongly linked to the pervious elements. In fact, Nurturing is an important element that acts as a catalyst in regard to engaging your team.

You may use the following "Action Time" to co-create an instant, elegant development plan for each of your direct reports.

It includes four parts: set long-term career goals, set medium-term goals, set short-term goals, and roadmap to achieve the set goals.

Set Long-Term Goals (5 Years)

These long-term goals (5+ years' time frame) represent the team member's overall career goals, may be even beyond their tenure at your organisation.

For instance, a long-term career goal for a manager in the technology industry might be, "To be recognised in software industry as a Chief Technology Officer (CTO)."

Set Medium-Term Goals (2 Years)

These medium-term goals (2+ year time frame) represent the team member's career goals, usually within the tenure at your organisation.

For instance, a medium-term career goal for a manager in technology industry might be

- To be a recognised expert in the company for one of the technology verticals.
- To get a promotion to the role of "Chief Engineer– Technology" for one of the verticals of the company.
- To get hands on experience in handling nationwide projects.

Set Short-Term Goals (6 Months)

Short term goals (which typically have a 6 month+ timeframe) help a team member achieve his or her long-term and medium objectives, while helping the organisation achieve its goals. You work with the team member to arrive at goals that meet the above objective.

Roadmap to Achieve Goals

The plan describes how the team member will achieve his or her goals. It includes some or all of the following:

- Assignments and challenges that will help the team member grow and get results.
- People, mentors, and new relationships that can help the team member succeed.
- Feedback and advice that will help the team member become more effective and learn how others perceive him or her.

- Formal training programmes and conferences to make new contacts and learn.
- Affiliations and networks.
- Reading and self-study.
- Other resources that can help.

You can decide to create a road map for a specific time frame. We suggest you create a six-month road map and review it every quarter.

Action Time: Development Plan

	6 Months+	2 Year+	5 Year+
Development Goals			
Success/ Performance goals			
Career goals			

Development Goals	6 Months+	2 Year+	5 Year+
Projects goals			
Organisational initiative goals			
Behavioural goals			
Skill goals			

Development Goals	6 Months+	2 Year+	5 Year+
Knowledge goals			
Professional certification goals			
Networking goals			
Any other?			

Create your road-map for six months (or more) to achieve above goals:

Action Time: Development Roadmap

Activity	Details	People who can help	Target date
New relationships to be created			
Personal branding to be changed / created			
Training sessions needed			

Mentoring required and from whom?		
Coaching required and areas to be coached		
Any professional courses / certifications to be done?		
Any feedback that will help?		

Let us understand the "Action Time" for Development Planning.

DESCRIPTION Action Time: Development Plan	
Parameter	**Description**
Success/ Performance Goals	Help your team member fill the success criteria/performance goals for the stipulated period.
Career Goals	Discuss and note the role or position that your team member would want to reach during the stipulated period.
Projects Goals	Are there any projects he/she wants to be part of in the mentioned development period?
Organisational initiative Goals	Please note down, any organisational initiatives they may want to be part of, during the development period.
Behavioural Goals	What are the behaviours he/she wants to change in the given period? What are the new behaviours he/she would like to acquire in the development period?
Skill Goals	What new skills (such as project management, product marketing etc.) does the team member want to achieve?
Knowledge Goals	What new subjects does the team member want to learn?
Professional Certification Goals	Are there any certifications that will enhance their capabilities and professionalism? Do such certificates help your team member gain "Expert" status and improve their standing in the organisation?
Networking Goals	Who all do they want to get connected to? How can you help them improve their visibility?
Any Other?	Anything else that comes up during the discussion.

DESCRIPTION

Action Time: Development Roadmap

Activity	Details	People who can help	Target date
New relationships to be created	Identify people with whom the team member should get connected.	Identify the people who can help for each specific activity. The people could be other team members, the HR team, other teams, the leadership team or even industry professionals.	Set a date for the completion of the activity.
Personal branding to be changed/ created	Identify what image the team member wishes to have. Help identify the gaps and opportunities to improve or modify the image. It could be presentation opportunities to the senior leadership or to the end customer, or representation of the company at the industry forums.		
Training sessions needed	Any training that aligns with the skill development needs of the individual.		

Mentoring required and from whom?	Based on the individual's professional development plans, please identify a leader from the relevant domain who could mentor and provide some opportunities to learn through small assignments.
Coaching required and areas to be coached	In case the individual can benefit from regular coaching interventions to achieve his / her goals, it may be worthwhile assigning a coach. This is especially applicable to high potential individuals, who work hard and are capable of fast growth. The growth of such individuals into the leaders of tomorrow shall be beneficial to the company.
Any professional courses / certifications to be done?	Identify professional certifications that will help in skill development as well as establishing credibility of the individual as an expert in his/her desired field of study.
Any feedback that will help?	Please setup regular feedback sessions to help the individual to keep moving in the right direction.

Below are listed a few things that you should take care of when having the development discussions, these guidelines are simple and effective, and help make the discussion more fruitful.

Say Less of...	Say More of...
Yes, but...	Let's see how we can...
This is a waste of time. Let's get to the bottom line...	Let's see what's possible...

Do Less of	Do More of
Close minded...	Open discussions
Fear of mistakes	Learning from mistakes
Fear of giving too much freedom	Opening boundaries and encouraging engagement

Day 148: The story continues

Arun is excited about looking at the final element of the HUMAN framework. He has been on this journey with Rohit for the past five months and has seen a change not only in his engagement with each of his team members but also in the way he feels about his own job.

He is more confident at being able to work with people.

Rohit encourages Arun to look at the "Action Time" for "Nurturing" and to complete it for his team members.

Arun's organisation has individual development plans as part of their appraisal cycle. Arun gets these details from HR. He understands that the formal process provides for one-time creation of the development plan during the performance cycle. He familiarises himself with the all the training and development options available to him for his team.

He starts with Ashok, and works with him to complete his development plan. He takes a look back at the previous HUMAN elements as well to support his ideas. He finds compared to other exercises that he has completed with Ashok, this time it is a much easier discussion because they share a far better relationship.

Team Member Name: Ashok			
Action Time: Development Plan			
Development goals	6 Months +	2 Year +	5 Year +
Success/ performance goals	To deliver the current project successfully.	To develop his team with respect to technical knowledge.	TBD (To be Done)
Career goals	-	To become Project Director.	TBD
Projects goals	-	To work on one overseas project.	TBD
Organisational initiative goals	-	To be a part of the mentoring initiatives and mentor one person.	TBD
Behavioural goals	Develop listening skills.	Improve collaboration and communication skills.	TBD
Skill goals	Interpersonal communication.	Presentation skills.	TBD
Knowledge goals	Domain knowledge for banking sector.	Learn about automation.	TBD
Professional certification goals	Project Management Professional (PMP) certification.	TBD	TBD
Networking goals	Form better relationships with all direct reports.	Create visibility with two overseas Project Directors.	TBD
Any other?	-	-	-

219

Action Time: Development Roadmap			
Activity	**Details**	**People who can help**	**Target date**
New relationships to be created	Form relationships with direct reports. Develop relationships with two overseas directors.	Arun	3 months 1 year
Personal branding to be changed / created	Not Applicable	Not Applicable	Not Applicable
Training sessions needed	Interpersonal skills.	L&D Department	6 months-1 year
Mentoring required and from whom?	Ashok wants to be mentored by Anupam.	Arun, Anupam	1 year
Coaching required and areas to be coached	Not Applicable	Not Applicable	Not Applicable
Any professional courses/ certifications to be done?	Project Management Professional (PMP) certification.	Self	8 months
Any feedback that will help?	Feedback from Arun and Anupam on performance.	Arun, Anupam, Ashok	6 months

Since, it was a first such meeting, Arun could not cover all of the topics, especially the ones that looked at the long term plan. Part of the reason was that Ashok never had the opportunity to discuss and think about his own development plans. Arun realised that it will take more than one meeting to refine and finalise the plans, but they now had enough to go on and many actions are already decided for the coming months. He puts down into his calendar a specific time for discussion with Ashok for three months later and commits to a systematic review. He reminds himself that team members may often neglect their own development; he looks at his own journey following the HUMAN framework and all the learning that he got from over past 5 months. He is extremely grateful to Rohit to have not just provided the knowledge, but all the motivation as well the occasional nudge or push which helped him overcome his inertia or hesitations. He resolves that his team deserved no less, and that it is his duty to return the favour and propagate the knowledge to being a great leader.

Arun reflects on the element Nurturing and feels that it is a natural extension to all that he has learned in the HUMAN framework. He looks forward to meeting other team members and helping to create their own personal development plans.

Conclusion

"Well begun is half done."

-Aristotle

Conclusion

It has been seven months since Arun started working with the HUMAN framework. The initial hiccups and coming to terms with his own approach did take a little time but he has been finally able to overcome issues and align himself with the HUMAN framework. He is doing well with his team and project.

Here is an excerpt from one of his discussions with Rohit.

Rohit: How are you feeling today after practising HUMAN for seven months?

Arun: I am feeling good, proud of myself and I know that though I have already benefitted, I can continue to benefit even more from it, since the framework gives us endless potential. I have been appreciated by Anupam and the on-site team.

Rohit: What are the components of the framework which have worked the best for you?

Arun: Actually, everything worked. It looked like a lot of hard work to the techie in me, but the framework breaks down the whole issue into smaller components. This is exactly like handling one component at a time in a tangible manner and that's an easy thing to do. After doing this for some time now, I feel quite aligned with the process.

Rohit: I am happy that you liked it and it has worked well, but still would you like to reflect on what worked the best for you?

Arun: "The first piece" connecting to self, being self-aware has worked for me the best, I believe. Now I am more aware as a person. I have been successfully able to change a couple of my behaviours. I could not have achieved this without the framework helping me. Also, the step-by-step process of understanding the team has worked wonders as I didn't know so much about my team before.

Rohit: That is really good. What part has been most challenging?

Arun: Messaging, I still struggle with it. I am working on that part. Still I feel that I need to be more aware of the Messaging aspect when I talk to my team. I believe I must practice it more.

Rohit: What kind of impact did it have on delivery?

Arun: By using the HUMAN framework, I have reached a stage where most of the project deliverables are on time now. Sub-teams are communicating with each other. They have now got somebody in common to talk to and that's me. Teams are raising their concerns on time, so issues are getting resolved in time.

Rohit: Did it have any kind of impact on you as an individual?

Arun: Certainly, I have become more aware, caring and understanding. I listen better and if I don't, I know it now. I am aware of my communication style with the team; I try to relate it to the Messaging part of the HUMAN framework and I am still learning that aspect. Also, I had never thought of Acknowledging people in such a structured fashion. The structure has helped me to understand and acknowledge everybody in the right way.

I now see a path to my team becoming quite independent and I hope that in future, I will get more time for my own development. HUMAN has shown me possibilities of a fast track career growth. I intend to continue to practice it.

Frankly there is also an effect on me in my personal life. I have started becoming aware of my behaviours at home too.

Rohit: What is the next level you want to achieve on team engagement?

Arun: I want to practice it more and want a 100% positive feedback from my team in the next five months. By that time, it will be a year of practicing HUMAN. I also want to work more on the Nurturing and Messaging part.

Rohit: How would you summarise your learning about engagement?

Arun: I have learnt that:

- Engagement is a journey, not a destination. It is continuous. Still my team gets disengaged at times but our communication and behaviour have become much better. So, our problems are not that major now.
- I need to be engaged to engage my team in the right way.
- It is all about being more connected to each team member at their level and all of us coming together for a bigger purpose.

Rohit: Would you recommend this framework to somebody else in your organisation?

Arun: Oh yes, I want to recommend this to all my direct reports. They should also use this framework to engage their teams and be more connected. If all of us work in a similar fashion, there will be more synergies and a better connect from top to bottom and vice versa.

Day 250: A Call for Celebration

After one more month, Arun invited Rohit for sharing his progress and for celebrating his success so far.

Rohit congratulated Arun and appreciated his dedication.

Arun makes it a point to meet Rohit once in one month to discuss his reflections and his challenges with the HUMAN framework. He now talks about the team in a positive manner and sounds motivated and engaged.

HUMAN makes a difference

You may have observed from the story that Arun has come a long way in a short period of eight months despite the fact that he was struggling with his project and his team. Also, note that he was new to the company and the project and it was the first time that he was having senior people in his team. He was under significant pressure to improve the situation and the HUMAN framework helped him achieve success under difficult circumstances. The HUMAN framework is designed as a systematic solution; it brings in a lot of objectivity and is a great fit for technology leaders.

The HUMAN framework is based on basic human traits, so once you start, slowly it shows up in your behaviours. The structured "Action Time" will ensure that you are really onto it and that you are not losing sight of what you plan. You can keep building on what you have already done despite the daily fire-fighting at work. It nicely fits along with the usual fire-fighting process. It will help you to transform yourself into a people's person, a true leader who takes his/her team along.

Once it shows up in your behaviours, you will tend to have better relationships beyond your team, i.e. with other stakeholders too. When you practice Messaging, Acknowledgement etc., with your team, your mental patterns will train you to be thoughtful of all these elements with other people in your life too. As this framework works on the basic human traits, it is going to be a helpful tool for you to be an effective leader, effective colleague and more effective in your relationships outside the office as well.

What is the Next Step?

The next step is to make a commitment, a commitment to yourself, your team, your business, with the most important commitment being to yourself. It is a beautiful journey of self-discovery, and like all discoveries there will be both joy and despair. Remain focused on your goals and the change you want to bring, and keep going, your rewards will be endless.

Are you ready? Please go to Chapter 2 and start practicing.

Should you need support you may also write to us on **leaderyouwanttobe@rootz.co.in** to seek any help on the framework.

We are confident that your journey will be well worth your effort. We wish you a lot of success.

APPENDIX - 1

Value chart (Not an exhaustive list)

Accountability	Control	Equality
Accuracy	Cooperation	Excellence
Achievement	Correctness	Excitement
Adventurousness	Courtesy	Expertise
Ambition	Creativity	Exploration
Assertiveness	Curiosity	Expressiveness
Balance	Decisiveness	Fairness
Being the best	Democraticness	Faith
Belonging	Dependability	Fidelity
Boldness	Determination	Fitness
Calmness	Diligence	Fluency
Carefulness	Discipline	Focus
Challenge	Discretion	Freedom
Cheerfulness	Diversity	Fun
Commitment	Dynamism	Generosity
Community	Economy	Grace
Compassion	Effectiveness	Growth
Competitiveness	Efficiency	Happiness
Consistency	Empathy	Hard
Contentment	Enjoyment	Work
Contribution	Enthusiasm	Health

Helping	Openness	Simplicity
Society	Order	Soundness
Honesty	Originality	Speed
Honour	Patriotism	Spontaneity
Humility	Perfection	Stability
Independence	Devotion	Strategic
Ingenuity	Positivity	Strength
Inner Harmony	Practicality	Structure
Inquisitiveness	Preparedness	Success
Insightfulness	Professionalism	Support
Intelligence	Prudence	Teamwork
Intellectual	Quality-orientation	Thankfulness
Status	Reliability	Thoroughness
Intuition	Resourcefulness	Thoughtfulness
Joy	Restraint	Timeliness
Justice	Results-oriented	Tolerance
Leadership	Rigor Security	Traditionalism
Legacy	Self-actualization	Trustworthiness
Love	Self-control	Truth-seeking
Loyalty	Selflessness	Understanding
Making a difference	Self-reliance	Uniqueness
Mastery	Sensitivity	Unity
Merit	Serenity	Usefulness
Obedience	Service	Victory

Manbir Kaur

 Manbir is an Executive and Leadership Coach (Professional Certified Coach, PCC-ICF). She is also a Conversational Intelligence(C-IQ) Enhanced Practitioner.

She specializes in coaching leaders from technology organisations. Her clients include executives from various technology companies from India, UK, US, Middle East etc.

Over years she has developed specific frameworks for technology organisations. Her frameworks make coaching progress "measurable" and she has pioneered methods to make sure that her clients can evaluate the ROI of the engagement.

She has more than two decades of work experience. Prior to being a coach, Manbir has worked in corporate world for various Indian and Multinational IT companies in roles such as Development, Operations, Presales, People Management and Consulting.

Currently, She, also serves on the Board of ICF Delhi NCR Chapter.

Authors can be reached at: *leaderyouwanttobe@rootz.co.in*

FB resource page:

https://www.facebook.com/Areyoutheleaderyouwanttobe/ offers additional tools and information for the readers. It is the platform where you can interact with authors and other readers.

Kathy Mitchell

Kathy has over 25 years' experience in the field of human resources, training, and leadership and people development in both the corporate and public sectors in diversely different locations in the world.

Over the course of her professional career, she has assumed many leadership roles as a Human Resources and Leadership Development professional in Royal Dutch Shell, Human Resources Advisor in the United Nations for the Cambodian Mine Action Centre and Naval Officer &Training and Development specialist for the Royal Australian Navy. In her current role, she is an independent Leadership Development Coach and Facilitator, based in Kuala Lumpur, Malaysia.

She has a Master's Degree in Adult Education and is a Certified Professional Coach (CPC) through the Corporate Coach Academy, Malaysia and an internationally recognized Associate Certified Coach (ACC) through the International Coach Federation (ICF). She is also a Conversational Intelligence (C-IQ) Enhanced Practitioner.

Authors can be reached at: *leaderyouwanttobe@rootz.co.in*

FB resource page:
https://www.facebook.com/Areyoutheleaderyouwanttobe/
offers additional tools and information for the readers. It is the platform where you can interact with authors and other readers.

Other #SMBooks

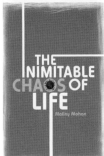

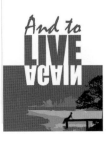

Other #SMBooks

"The Un-Parenting Guide"

DONT RAISE
YOUR CHILDREN
RAISE YOURSELF

DR.SWATI LODHA
www.drswatilodha.com

MERAKI

Hana Vaid

OSWALD PEREIRA

GOLMAAL in Goa

KNOCKED OUT
A crispy punch of Love

SABI SHAIKH

Book one of
THE KEY SERIES
Lost - The Capture

LULIANA MARTINI

AKSHARAA AGARWAL

Treacherous
Desires

Kritika Sharma

SOLITUDE
REVISITED
MANASWITA GHOSH

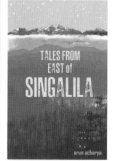

TALES FROM
EAST of
SINGALILA

arun acharya

INVERTED
Unobvious reflections towards a better life

ARVIND BHANDARI

A Bride,
A Murder
& A Trail of Blood

Promises of
a firefly

ANUPAM PATRA

A sip of Love &
A sip of Coffee

Ganga Bharani

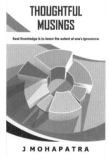

THOUGHTFUL
MUSINGS

Real Knowledge is to know the extent of one's ignorance

J MOHAPATRA

Simplify
your
Life

VAIBHAV DATAR

Feathers
& Fire
Pakhi Dixit

9 Chocolatey
Bites
A Short Story
Collection
for Children

The Messy Desk
A Trail of Laddoos
The Mango Pickle
My Secret Scribes

Ananya V. Ganesh